Young Writers 2005

PLAYGRO

Let your creativity flow...

ode
limerick haiku
rhyme
ballad

Southern Counties Vol II
Edited by Steve Twelvetree

 Young**Writers**

First published in Great Britain in 2005 by:
Young Writers
Remus House
Coltsfoot Drive
Peterborough
PE2 9JX
Telephone: 01733 890066
Website: www.youngwriters.co.uk

SB ISBN 1 84602 270 3

Foreword

Young Writers was established in 1991 and has been passionately devoted to the promotion of reading and writing in children and young adults ever since. The quest continues today. Young Writers remains as committed to the fostering of burgeoning poetic and literary talent as ever.

This year's Young Writers competition has proven as vibrant and dynamic as ever and we are delighted to present a showcase of the best poetry from across the UK. Each poem has been carefully selected from a wealth of *Playground Poets* entries before ultimately being published in this, our thirteenth primary school poetry series.

Once again, we have been supremely impressed by the overall high quality of the entries we have received. The imagination, energy and creativity which has gone into each young writer's entry made choosing the best poems a challenging and often difficult but ultimately hugely rewarding task - the general high standard of the work submitted amply vindicating this opportunity to bring their poetry to a larger appreciative audience.

We sincerely hope you are pleased with our final selection and that you will enjoy *Playground Poets Southern Counties Vol II* for many years to come.

Contents

Robert D Morgan (10)	19
Naomi Hayman (10)	19
Gemma Folland (10)	20
Charlie Hames (10)	20
Gemma Crosbie (10)	21
Louise Dawson (11)	21
Sinead Gulless (10)	22
George Stott (11)	23
Tom Saunders (11)	23
Jonathon Moss (9)	24
Amie Mason (9)	24
Morgan Chmielewski (11)	24
Daniel Shears (9)	25

Chilton Primary School, Ramsgate

Benjy Cohen (10)	25

Cookham Rise Primary School, Cookham

Andrew Mack (11)	26
Laura Tull (11)	27
Jodie Macfarren (11)	28
Rebecca Brayne (11)	29
Naomi Rawlinson (11)	30
Samantha Dance (11)	31
Danielle Rickard (10)	32
Daniel John (11)	33
Kane Rose (11)	34
Sharmaine Hughes (11)	35
Justin James (11)	35
Rebecca Curley (11)	36
Charlotte Boulton (10)	36
Clara Millar (11)	37
Mark Wilson (11)	37
Philip Hellmuth (11)	38

Drapers Mills CP School, Margate

Maddison Heskett (9)	38
Shannon Murray (9)	39
Sarah Galbraith (9)	39
Charlotte Stratton (9)	40

Shorab Dey (9)   40
Scarlett Preston (8)   41
Laura Myers (9)   41
Bryn Llewellyn (9)   42
Lucy Bailey (9)   42
Charnice Maxted (8)   43
Steven Taylor (10)   43
Shannon Parker (9)   44
Abigail Davies (9)   44
Katie Rogers (9)   45
Gavin Ward (8)   45
Anna Harris (9)   46
Anna Flood (9)   46
Ashley Cole (9)   47
Rachel Louise Buckley (10)   48
Sandra Nightingale (9)   49
Louise Dignam (10)   49
Daniel Galbraith (9)   50
Daniella Rossiter (10)   50
Victoria Reason (9)   51
Rees Peterson (10)   51

East Preston Junior School, East Preston

Sam Gilbert (11)   52
Brett Pine (10)   52
Victoria Balsdon (11)   53
Eden Smith (11)   53
Ben Cripps (11)   54
Alastair Finlinson & Luke Bridger (11)   54
Lauren Andrews (11)   55
Maddie Moore (10)   55
Eddie Blandamer (11)   56
Anastasia Perysinakis (8)   56
Emma Withers (11)   57
Jamie Worsa (11)   58
Chris Moore (11)   58
Aisha Cove (8)   59
Harry Forrest (9)   59
Leah Childs (9)   60
Gary Burger (11)   61
Connor Mott (9)   62

Foxborough Primary School, Slough

Georgian Gardens CP School, Rustington

Nicole Pearce (11)   82
Louis Valentine (10)   82
Ben West (10)   83
Danielle Brown (10)   83
Harriet Mayhead (10)   84
Antonia Lunn (11)   84

Holyport CE Primary School, Holyport
Samah Hussain (8)   85
Philippa Bailey (10)   85
Jade Hill (8)   86

Kingsclere CE Primary School, Kingsclere
Jake Sellwood (11)   86
Rupert Broad (10)   87
Hannah Martin & Marianne Borzoni (10)   88
Jonathan Cotter (10)   88
Hannah Bright & Pippa Allwood (10)   89
Ben Rampton & Nicholas Jenkins (10)   90
George Caren & Imogen Brown (11)   91

Leigh Primary School, Tonbridge
Louise Knapp (10)   91
Ellie Warr (11)   92
Shannon Reid (11)   93
Anna Chapman (11)   94
Sarah-Jane Levings (11)   94

Licensed Victuallers' School, Ascot
Chloe Foster (10)   95
James Chapman (10)   96
Tim Allison (10)   97
Edward Slegg (10)   98
Becky Stark (10)   99
Hattie Price (10)   100

Lytchett Matravers Primary School, Poole
Sadie Banyard (11)   100
Lauren Murray (10)   101
Victoria Day (11)   101

Micklands Primary School, Caversham

Napier CP School, Gillingham

Northolmes Junior School, Horsham

Shauna Mansbridge (11)	124
Daniel Randon (11)	125
Aaron Czajkowska (11)	125
Nicole Barnes (11)	126
Emma Rickman (11)	126
Lauren Jones (11)	127
Chloe Fletcher (11)	127
Matthew Trotman (11)	127
Jamie-Leigh Price (11)	128
Emma Hollingworth (11)	128
Lauren Hale (10)	129
Rebecca Loughnane (11)	129
Alice Jarvis (10)	130
Devon Watson (11)	131
Sophie Lebba (12)	131
Christopher Cakebread (10)	132
Oliver Salmon (11)	132
Ross Walden (11)	133
Chelsea Johnson (11)	133
Jessica Ball (10)	134
Rebecca Rickman (11)	134
Louise Barnard (11)	135
Katie Heath (10)	135
Lucy Martlew (11)	136
Jake Gallard (11)	136
Josh Tustin (11)	136
Dan Maguire (10)	137
Matthew Morrison (11)	137
Laura Hollobon (10)	138
Aaron Moss (11)	138
Ciara Spence (11)	138

St Catherine's RC Primary School, Bridport

Nicholas Roberts (9)	139
Eleanor Reynolds-Grey (9)	139
Cameron Taylor (9)	140
Troy Smith (8)	141
Beth Donovan (9)	141
Luke Antinoro (10)	142
Alexandra Blanchard (9)	142

Rory Smith (10)   143
Robert Evans (10)   143
Joseph Grew-McEvoy (9)   144
Michael Brown (9)   144
Leticia Ebben (10)   145
Oliver Hibbs (10)   145
Charlie Teideman (9)   146
Sophie Hall (9)   146
Lottie Woolner (10)   147
Ned Parmiter (10)   147
Katherine Crabb (10)   148
Harriet Stanley (10)   148
Gabrielle Horton (10)   148
Phillippa Gatehouse (9)   149
Rosemary Shearman (9)   149
Thomas Grogan (9)   150
Edward Whitehead (10)   150
Alice Budden (9)   150

St Catherine's RC Primary School, Littlehampton

Zaccarie Tregarthen-Riley (7)   151
Katie McIlwain (8)   151
Michelle Solomon (8)   151
Melanie Martin (8)   152
Michael Dorey (8)   152
Daniel Burdfield (8)   152
Sean Ayling (8)   153
Archie Mustow (8)   153
Jake Davies (8)   153
Hana-Lina Kasujja (8)   154
Abigail Blondell (8)   154
Braden Kenny (8)   154
Siobhan Maysey (8)   155
Lucie Derrick (8)   155

Salmestone Primary School, Margate

Brittany Wilson (7)   155

Sibertswold CE Primary School, Shepherdswell

Tom Harman (9)	156
Jacob Roberts (8)	156
Ruby Russell (9)	157
Brandon Forrest (8)	157
Annabel Reville (9)	158
Alex Hamby (9)	159
Charlotte Powell (9)	159
Claire Penny (8)	160
Laura Palmer (9)	160
Chloe Peerless (9)	161
Alexi Payne (9)	161
Abigail McLean (9)	162
Harry Moore (9)	162
George Fordham (9)	163
Nicholas Dray (9)	163
Lucy Gilchrist (9)	164
Alice Heath (10)	164
Laura Castledine (8)	165
Luke Firth-Coppock (9)	165
Hannah Coupe (8)	166
Shannah Hall (9)	166
Molly Billington (8)	167
Brandon Faulkner (9)	168

South Stoke Primary School, South Stoke

Max Brown (10)	168
George Scholey (11)	169
Eloise Craven-Todd (11)	169
Kimberley Ambler (11)	169
Oliver Craven-Todd (9)	170
Grace Beacham-Vickery (11)	170
Joseph Kitt (10)	171
Scott Harwood (10)	171
Rebecca Stevens (10)	171
Harry Haslam (11)	172

Spinners Acre Junior School, Chatham

Georgia Stevenson (8)	172
Ryan Catt (8)	173

Sarah Dormand (10)	189
Ayesha Mahmood (9)	190
Alisha Panue (9)	190
Jack Waite (11)	190
Henry Warren (11)	191
Lucy Smith (11)	191
Anagha Sharma (8)	192

Stourfield Junior School, Bournemouth

Oonagh Fox (10)	192
Lucy Pennick (11)	193
Alexander Travis (10)	193
Alice Brown (11)	193
Lydia Smith (11)	194
Sarah Kearsey (10)	194
Tom Hall (11)	195
Jay Branch (12)	195
Jason Brown-Burt (11)	195
Gregory Roy (10)	196
Benedict Petch (11)	196
Hannah Daykin (11)	197
James Diffey (11)	197
Alana Strutt (10)	197
Sian Scorer (11)	198
Ryan Galpin (11)	198
Claudia Welcome (10)	198

Whitehill Junior School, Gravesend

Georgina Ralph (10)	199
Shannon Firth (11)	200
Lauren Perkins (11)	200
Matthew Martin (10)	201
Chloe Stannard (11)	201
Liam Ives (11)	202
Reece Gregory (11)	202
Tia Tia (11)	203
Aaron Merton (10)	203
Nafi Asova (11)	204
Jimmy Acott (10)	204
Jordan Weller (11)	205
Chris Trimming (11)	205

The Poems

The Lost Shoe

This shoe has been worn by hundreds of people,
It's been through long, lush, green grass,
It's been on muddy walks squelching all the time.
This shoe has been worn for sports,
It's been used for football, tennis, even basketball,
It's been up trees and in classrooms.
This shoe has been threatened,
It has run for its life and jumped in the river to save itself,
It's been on sandy beaches with palm trees,
It's been in the Arctic on ice,
But now I've lost it forever,
The shoe I named Trevor.

Samantha Harper (11)
Balcombe CE Primary School, Balcombe

Have You Ever Seen?

(Poem using homophones)

Have you ever seen a riverbank store any money?
Or water tanks shoot down planes
With their armour-piercing bullets?
Has a herd of sheep ever stopped to listen
Or has a box ever won a boxing match?
Why can't a leak solve starvation?
And how come a metal bar can't serve me a pint?
I wonder what wood chips taste like with salt and vinegar?
And why don't baseball bats hang in dark, dark caves?

Oscar Woolgar (11)
Balcombe CE Primary School, Balcombe

Kennings

Tree-waster
Page-stapler
Ink-user
Bookmark-loser
Strong-back
Information-stack
Fun-provider
Page-divider
Catching-blurb
Sometimes-absurd
Maybe-pretending
Happy-ending
What am I?

Ellen Hill (10)
Balcombe CE Primary School, Balcombe

What Am I?

Whipper-snapper
Human-attacker
Bone-crusher
Roaring-rusher
River-waiter
Unsinkable-hater
What am I?

Owen Bisman (10)
Balcombe CE Primary School, Balcombe

The Life Of A Library Book

(Based on a poem by Brian Moses)

This library book has seen many young faces.
Its pages have been turned thousands of times,
And have come very close to being ripped.
This library book has been lost,
And felt neglected and lonely.
It has been on countless car journeys and holidays.
This library book has had its spine broken.
It has been dropped in dirty puddles,
And nearly drowned.
This library book has made children laugh for hours.
It has made them excited and is filled with suspense.
No one ever puts it down.
This library book now lies on a dusty shelf.
It is now an unpopular book.
No one even gives it a look.

Dan Hill (10)
Balcombe CE Primary School, Balcombe

Happiness

Happiness is yellow like a cheerful, warm sun.
It tastes like sweet, ripe strawberries and cream.
It looks like a joyful smile raised upon a poor child's face.
It feels like soft velvet, warm and comforting.
It reminds me of a picnic with all my family.
It sounds like a beautiful nightingale singing in a silver tree.
It smells like a dozen sweet-scented roses
Wafting around on the warm, evening breeze.

Kathryn Beckett (11)
Balcombe CE Primary School, Balcombe

Titanic Poem

(Inspired by 'Casabianca' by Felicia Hemans)

The day Papa left was a dreadful day,
Full of sorrow all the way.
I looked for him amidst the Titanic,
He wasn't there, I began to panic.
Papa was the only one,
Without him my life was gone.

The mighty ship had split in half,
I heard the sound of a drunken man having a laugh.
But what was funny? Had he gone mad?
Papa was dead and all was sad.
Debris splayed haphazardly,
Bodies floated on the ice-cold sea.

All was lost amongst the wreckage,
I was left with but a message:
Papa told me to save my own life,
Don't look back for fear of strife.
I floated away on the lifeboat,
Covered in Papa's favourite coat.

All is now blanked from my memory,
Papa dead in the Atlantic sea.

Joe Bolland (11)
Balcombe CE Primary School, Balcombe

Nonsense

(Poem using homophones)

Has a pencil ever been lead?
Have you ever seen a flower in a bed?
Have you ever seen an oak tree bark
Or have you ever seen a knight in the dark?
Have you ever seen your mummy woken from her sleep?
Does water ever come dripping out from a leek?

Joanne James (11)
Balcombe CE Primary School, Balcombe

What Am I?

Child-climber
Leaf-flyer
Blossom-flinger
Root-clinger
Branch-breaker
Twig-maker
Nest-provider
Water-inside her
Buds-popping
Leaves-flopping
What am I?

Lucy Erin Backley (11)
Balcombe CE Primary School, Balcombe

Who Am I?

Cattle-rider
Food-provider
Sheep-herder
Pig-murderer
Chicken-feeder
Horse-keeper
Cow-milker
Fox-killer
Who am I?

Brett Pointing (11)
Balcombe CE Primary School, Balcombe

What Am I?

My name is Sam,
I hiss, I bite and you see me at night.
I have a long tail and lots of scales.
I eat mice and they taste pretty nice.
I also eat eggs but I have no legs.
When on land I live in sand,
I can swim but I find it grim.
    What am I?

Sophie Harper (11)
Balcombe CE Primary School, Balcombe

What Am I?

I swing from tree to tree,
Looking at the ground beneath me,
A sudden flicker and I'm gone,
Through the forest where I belong,
Living on the forest fruits,
Nuts and bugs, leaves and roots,
I'm rather like you and I,
But I'm more reclusive and shy,
    What am I?

David Rusden (11)
Balcombe CE Primary School, Balcombe

What Am I?

A rubbish muncher
A tin can cruncher
A home cleaner
A garbage eater
A fly attractor
A waste food extractor
What am I?

Sam Hazelden (10)
Balcombe CE Primary School, Balcombe

What Am I?

Mouse catcher
Bird snatcher
Great pouncer
Marvellous-bouncer
I play
All day
Never stopping
Always flopping
What am I?

Chloe Turner (11)
Balcombe CE Primary School, Balcombe

What Am I?

Clicker-clacker
Metal-cracker
Home-wrecker
Target-tracker
Distant-killer
Blood-spiller
Stealth-hider
What am I?

Jake Godfrey (10)
Balcombe CE Primary School, Balcombe

Silence

Silence is like the whiteness of a dove,
It reminds me of my first time getting grounded.
It smells like a field of freshly cut grass.
Silence looks like a room full of children doing their SATs.
It sounds like trees swaying in the breeze.
Sometimes silence feels like your voice has been imprisoned.

George Searl (11)
Balcombe CE Primary School, Balcombe

What Am I?

I am blue, I rule the sea,
The king of the ocean,
A mighty mammal.
I am bigger than a double-decker bus,
With a loud, proud wail.
The harmless animal
And the hunter's victim,
Eating plankton.
What am I?

Ella Robertson (10)
Balcombe CE Primary School, Balcombe

Hickory Dickory Dock
(Based on 'Nursery Crimes' by Michael Rosen)

Hickory, dickory, dock,
The mouse was making a frock,
The clock struck one,
The dress was done,
Hickory, dickory, dock.

Matthew Daniel (11)
Balcombe CE Primary School, Balcombe

Bedtime Routine

Every night when I read
At the end of this I plead
Can I read just a little more?
Because bed's a God Almighty bore.
And I think it is agreed.

Lauren Pringle (9)
Branksome Heath Middle School, Poole

The Three Little Pigs

The big bad wolf overheard the pigs' mummy
He thought by Friday they would be in his tummy
He ran around, 'Hip hip hooray
I am going to eat them today!'

Meanwhile, the pigs happy in their homey
They were warm and cosy
One was straw with a yellow door
One in sticks
Another was bricks.

The first pig's home was made of straw
And it had a yellow door
It lives as happily as can be
Until suddenly
In comes Wolfy
In his tummy was the first little piggy.

The second had a house of sticks
And the little piggy inside kicks
He bursts in and gobbles him up
And he has a cup of tea
Then he needs a little wee.

Then he pays a visit to the pig that lives in bricks
This one also kicks
They play around all day long
Then the wolf got hit on the head
And so it is said
He was never heard of again.

Izabelle Thomas (9)
Branksome Heath Middle School, Poole

Living Colours

I start off as a little baby with all my family,
My mum looks after me like any other mum.
But when I am a few weeks old I see the sunlight for myself.
I am shooting up, my arms get longer,
My legs get longer but I cannot move.
Not long after you can see my eyes,
They may be any colour or rainbow-coloured.
I end up looking like a lion
But instead of scaring away the birds they come to me.
I have babies of my own now,
Some are close to me
But some are many miles away.
I will die soon but my children will still live.
They are a part of me so I will never properly go
And I will keep my colours until the day I die!

Vicky Olive (9)
Branksome Heath Middle School, Poole

Night Is Death

They're lurking somewhere
But you just don't know.
They feed on living souls, ripping flesh like starving tigers.
They come out on the midnight moon,
Limping in every direction.
They're coming after you . . .
And you know it now,
So just don't go clubbing at midnight
Or you might become a zombie!

James Taylor (9)
Branksome Heath Middle School, Poole

The Night Ghost

The man rode through the wood
In his dark black hood
The stars shone up high
As the horse galloped by
No one knew where he was going
He didn't want anyone knowing
He saw a fox and heard its cry
And then saw it run by
The stars were shut out by the trees
And then he felt a gentle breeze
Hours and hours of time went by
And then he gave a gentle sigh
The sun rose into the sky
And then he seemed to say goodbye
The sun's brightness shone
And then the man was gone
People say he'll come again
But no one seems to know when.

Menna Chmielewski (9)
Brightwalton CE Primary School, Newbury

My Cat's Death

Death will always come around,
When all life lets you down,
This sadly happened this very day,
When you tragically passed away.

We took you to the vets to see,
If you could stay and live with me.
You wouldn't make it, they put you down,
That very moment, without a sound.

2005 on the 14th May,
Gypsy the cat sadly passed away.

Nicola Barrie (11)
Brightwalton CE Primary School, Newbury

Death In The Old Barn

She breathed her last breath
It was her last moment
Her eyes grew wide
They were red with fear
With the queer moment of silence
A tear rolled down her cheek
She knew her killer was here
There was death all around her
Tied to the post
Her life flashing by
Outside the wind whistling in the trees
Outside the dark, spooky night
Her face was white
She was out of sight
Helpless
In the barn she hears
The sound of hay rustle
The creaks and whispers
As each tiny drop of sweat
Rolls down her ashen cheeks
The killer pulls out his gun
He pulls the trigger back
Out the bullet shoots
There was no turning back
Now she lays in the graveyard
Plotting as a ghost
Her revenge
On the stranger
Who shot her dead.

Rosanna Martin (11)
Brightwalton CE Primary School, Newbury

A Disastrous Holiday

I've had a disastrous holiday,
It started on the motorway,
Baby Kate screamed off her head,
And big sis Beth wished she was dead.

We drove all day on the motorway,
When suddenly the sky turned grey.

When we got to the holiday camp,
Our mobile home was wet and damp,
So we had to wait for hours and hours,
And from the clouds came murderous showers.

When we were ready the sky was black,
And the rain was dropping on my back.

I was up all night, all freezing cold,
And my duvet cover was covered in mould,
The very next day I fell out of bed,
I was battered and bruised and had hurt my head.

The rain was such an awful sight,
It carried on all day, all night.

This windy country, so full of gales,
This rainy country, it is called Wales,
I'll never ever go there again,
Next year I'll go to sunny Spain!

Stephanie Wilson (10)
Brightwalton CE Primary School, Newbury

The White Ghost

In the mist and the fog
Howls the howling dog
Next to the howling dog is a flint castle
In front of the castle was a white parcel

In the castle the parcel crept
In the coffin room it crept
It opened the coffin
To wake its friend

Inside the parcel was a white ghost
The ghost was a curse
Seeking for revenge

It went to the dungeon
To wake his friend
His friend was moaning and groaning

He went to the bedroom to open the cupboard
To wake his drooling friend

The three of them went down the corridor
Down the corridor they went
Their souls seeking for revenge
Down the corridor they went

They stepped outside
The sun melted them.

Hannah Booth (10)
Brightwalton CE Primary School, Newbury

A Windy Night

The raindrops fell to the ground far below,
And the plants and trees waved a scary hello.

The ground was muddy from the pouring rain,
And the horse that was riding could not take the pain.

He knew that his master was very close by,
Whistling loudly and giving a cry.

But the horse would not stop, turning back there was none,
And all the horse wished for was fresh grass and sun.

Suddenly a light went up in the sky,
And a roar of thunder crashed nearby.

His master was angry and that the horse knew,
His master got stronger as his temper grew.

This horse was strong and he wished to be free,
But his thoughts were disturbed as he crashed into a tree.

He twisted his ankle and hurt a front leg,
With the pain that he felt he wished he was dead.

This is the part where you really may cry,
For the pain had beaten him, the horse was to die.

As the horse passed away on this wet, muddy bed,
His master, the wind, took his spirit and fled!

Jenny Moss (11)
Brightwalton CE Primary School, Newbury

World War II

It was a normal day in 1939,
Everything was happy and fine,
When *boom, boom, boom,* they were coming,
The sound of soldiers' feet drumming.
'Pull out your guns,' shouted Captain Dain,
The bullet zinged by as he felt the pain.
Crash! He fell to the floor,
He was suffering, he could take no more.
'Get ready . . . *charge!*'
More soldiers would swoop in on their barge.
Soldiers on the ground, soldiers on the hilltops,
Soldiers everywhere.
Everyone would be aware.
It was silent and dark,
So silent you could hear in the distance a dog bark.
The war was over, finished and done with,
Only a few managed to live.
They had won the battle,
That few that were left climbed in their saddles.
They plodded away . . .
As the others would lay,
    In peace . . .

Amy Thornhill (11)
Brightwalton CE Primary School, Newbury

A Christmas Day

The robins are chirping,
As the bells are chiming.
Christmas is dawning,
As people are yawning.
Presents are opening,
As the wind is whistling.
Children are playing,
As the snow is laying.
Ice is freezing,
As the turkey is roasting.
People are singing,
As rabbits are running.
The kettle is boiling,
As the deer are calling.
Pheasants are flying,
The plants are dying.
Nothing is growing,
But the trees are blowing.
The sun is going,
As Christmas is ending.

Simon Morgan (11)
Brightwalton CE Primary School, Newbury

Ellie Jayne

Ellie Jayne,
    Plays in the rain,
        She is insane,
            She rides her Great Dane,
                Ellie Jayne,
                    Is a pain,
                        But she is my sister - I can't complain.

Emma Winstanley (11)
Brightwalton CE Primary School, Newbury

The Mysterious White Lady

The mysterious white lady lies in the bay,
She's in the dark alleyway.
The mysterious white lady's coming for the kill,
She's swooping over the window sill.
The mysterious white lady is very sly,
Every night she passes you by.
The mysterious white lady comes upstairs,
She will not answer any of your prayers.
The mysterious white lady comes into the room,
You will soon be facing your doom.
The mysterious white lady stabs you with a knife,
She has just ended your life.
The mysterious white lady has done her deed,
She has made your heart bleed and bleed.

Imogen Richards (10)
Brightwalton CE Primary School, Newbury

Winter

Winter's coming,
As autumn's leaving,
Trees are blowing,
Nothing growing.

Now it's raining,
The frost is freezing,
The snow is falling,
Christmas is calling.

Nights are drawing,
Children are moaning,
There is no playing,
As the snow is laying.

Ryan Collins (11)
Brightwalton CE Primary School, Newbury

The Otter's Journey

The otter's journey has just begun,
Jumping around, having fun,
Leaping over the rock and stones,
And hearing the heron's mournful moans.
The water flicking, splashing past,
And the silent vole swimming fast,
Swimming through river, place to place
Forever doing the river's race.

The fishes were leaping up and down,
As he saw the men from the town,
They took a shot,
To kill or not,
The bark of the hound,
Was the otter's last sound.
As in the river he lay,
And where he'll always stay.
His spirit's with the river fast,
His memory with the wind of past.

Robert D Morgan (10)
Brightwalton CE Primary School, Newbury

Jack

My pony Jack drinks Coke,
People think it is a joke.

Jack is grey,
He loves to eat hay.

Jack gets silly when it's time for food,
But most of the time he's really good.

I'd never swap him for any of the rest,
Even though he is a pest.

Naomi Hayman (10)
Brightwalton CE Primary School, Newbury

War Is Here

War is here, there are guns all around,
War is here, there's blood on the ground.
War is here, the bullets are fast,
War is here, my life is going past.

War is here, dead bodies everywhere,
War is here, I'm hiding in my lair.
War is here, undercover for years,
War is here, it hurts my ears.

War was here, I'm still alive,
War was here, I'm glad to survive.
War was here, everything is dead,
War was here, I've hurt my head.
War was here, I'm going to die,
War is over as down I lie!

Gemma Folland (10)
Brightwalton CE Primary School, Newbury

The War

The tanks hovered loudly by,
Armour gleaming brightly.
Their propelling jets burned
The golden fields of rye.
They launched their deadly raids,
Accurate and nightly.
The silent stealth bombers,
Gleaming white and blue,
Gave the deadly tankers,
Their dark and evil cue.
The tankers opened fire,
The city burned straight down,
The sound of the explosion,
Could be heard all around.

Charlie Hames (10)
Brightwalton CE Primary School, Newbury

The Spooky Night

James walked slowly through the woods,
He saw this rider with a black hood,
He was galloping on his horse,
Whose hooves hit the ground with a great force.

James followed the rider through the woods,
He didn't know if the idea was good,
He didn't know where it was leading to,
But he had to do what he had to do.
Then a wooden cottage came into view.

James made sure he wasn't seen,
But the black-hooded rider came to him,
Really scared, James ran away quick,
The man charged behind him, James felt sick.

James dashed into his house without delay,
And the black-hooded rider stomped away,
But he said he'd come back one day.

Gemma Crosbie (10)
Brightwalton CE Primary School, Newbury

Horses

Clip-clop, clip-clop, she's coming
Clip-clop, clip-clop, her rider's humming
Clip-clop, clip-clop, up and down
Clip-clop, clip-clop, she's heading for the town

Tick-tock, tick-tock, time's going
Tick-tock, tick-tock, she's slowing
Tick-tock, tick-tock, she's sleepy
Tick-tock, tick-tock, her rider's very creepy

Sh, sh, sh, sh, she's asleep
Sh, sh, sh, sh, she lays in a heap
Sh, sh, sh, sh, she's gone down
Sh, sh, sh, sh, she's reached the town.

Louise Dawson (11)
Brightwalton CE Primary School, Newbury

The Haunted House

One dark, spooky night
The bats try to bite.
They swoop round the haunted house,
An owl is looking for a mouse.
The house is surrounded by lots of trees,
Where the owls and bats eat the bees.
An earwig lives in the house of the ghosts,
Which will make you deaf if you boast.
Once a year the ghosts get mail,
But to deliver that mail they always fail.
The mailman came from London to the haunted house,
To find on the doorstep a dead mouse!
He'd scarcely knocked on the door,
The ghosts of course wanted more.
They wanted him to walk in,
And then be eaten with a glass of gin.
He saw the door open a crack,
So he thought he'd go in and have a snack.
So he walked in to see . . . what?
An earwig in a flowerpot.
The earwig emerged from his pot,
To see the mailman standing on his spot.
He draws nearer to the man,
With a giant pan.
He sticks the end of the pan in his ear,
Now he cannot hear.
Now the ghosts,
Have taught everyone not to boast!

Sinead Gulless (10)
Brightwalton CE Primary School, Newbury

Zululand!

The Zulus charged with their spears and shields,
Across all the fields.
The Red Coats' lines in order fired at will,
In an attempt to kill.
As the cannons fired,
The Zulus tired.
The Zulus fell one by one,
It was like slicing through a bun.
Suddenly out of nowhere,
Zulus were everywhere.
Reinforcements were issued soon,
Though the message did not get there until noon.
When the brigade finally arrived,
They realised no one had survived.

George Stott (11)
Brightwalton CE Primary School, Newbury

Road To Hell

Silently walking through the night,
Grant the killer saw a light.
The fences were rattling,
The dogs were howling.

Grant opened the door,
Walked across the floor.
He saw Terence lying there,
Slumped in his chair.

He fired a single shot,
It smashed a pot.
Terence knew it was his last second,
As Grant shot his last bullet.

Tom Saunders (11)
Brightwalton CE Primary School, Newbury

War Has Begun

War has begun so load your gun,
I'll tell you now it will not be fun,
War has begun so be afraid,
All the soldiers have begun to raid.

War has begun so go and hide,
If you want to live then stay by my side,
War has begun so if you're not fast,
Then your life will be passed.

Jonathon Moss (9)
Brightwalton CE Primary School, Newbury

The Horse In The Wood

There was once a horse in the wood,
He was eating grass all day.
When I went to see him,
He bucked and ran away.
I went over to the meadow,
He came running up to me.
I fed him a sugar lump,
And he thanked me for his tea.

Amie Mason (9)
Brightwalton CE Primary School, Newbury

Stranded!

The grass spikes his knees,
And his face is whipped by the breeze,
As the pollen wafts up his nose,
Torn are his ragged clothes,
His Spitfire lies in ruins,
Never shall it fly again.

Morgan Chmielewski (11)
Brightwalton CE Primary School, Newbury

Battle!

Gallop, gallop, gallop, we're riding into war,
Gallop, gallop, gallop, our gleaming horses roar,
Gallop, gallop, gallop, the horses are on the run,
Gallop, gallop, gallop, have you checked your guns?

March, march, march, watch out for troops,
March, march, march, see their shining boots,
March, march, march, get your guns set,
March, march, march, we'll win, you bet.

Bang, bang, bang, the guns have begun,
Bang, bang, bang, sounding like a badly-played drum,
Bang, bang, bang, oh no, I'm shot,
Bang, bang, bang, I'm bleeding a lot.

Ouch, ouch, ouch, I'm going to die,
Ouch, ouch, ouch, in the red-hot sky,
Ouch, ouch, ouch, the poppies will be popping up soon,
Ouch, ouch, ouch, my heart went *boom!*
　　Now I'm dead!

Daniel Shears (9)
Brightwalton CE Primary School, Newbury

Happiness

Happiness smells like rosemary in a summer breeze.
Happiness tastes like ready-made cake.
Happiness sounds like somebody laughing at the funniest thing.
Happiness looks like somebody smiling at their very best friend.
Happiness feels like running hot water coming out the bathroom taps.
Happiness reminds me of playing in Spain years ago.
Happiness is the colour of a new pink rose.

Benjy Cohen (10)
Chilton Primary School, Ramsgate

Andy's Magic Box

(Based on 'Magic Box' by Kit Wright)

I will put in the box . . .
The sweet taste of egg on toast in the morning
The scent of someone cooking breakfast in bed
The snowman left alone in the dark
And the noise of one million elephants.

I will put in the box . . .
The chocolate melting between your teeth
The smell of salty sea air
The sight of tears falling from your eyes
The feeling of the baby starting to kick
And the eardrum destroyed by the horn.

I will put in the box . . .
The hairs of man's best friend
Brushing against my face
Barking every night.

I will put in the box . . .
The heart belonging to the perfect girl
With the initials JM
I wish I could be
Together with her
Forever.

The fashion of the box is
A wooden box
A boring, old, wooden box
A broken, boring, old, wooden box
But it is never forgotten.

I will travel with my box
Through fire, seas and space
It carries my heart of family, friends and girlfriend
My box; my best friend.

Andrew Mack (11)
Cookham Rise Primary School, Cookham

Laura's Magic Box

(Based on 'Magic Box' by Kit Wright)

I will put in my box . . .
The feel of a newborn puppy
A book that my grandad gave me
A hot cup of tea that will forever stay hot

I will put in my box . . .
A picture of my family and friends
A scale from a terrifying dragon
A calming bird song

I will put in my box . . .
The taste of a Cadbury's chocolate bar
The smell of flowers
The smoothness of a stone

I will put in my box . . .
A flute playing softly
The smell of melting chocolate
My baby sister's very first smile

My box is made from
The greenest emerald
With some silver sparkles
To bring peace and luck wherever I go

I will take it everywhere
Till the day I die and beyond
Everywhere
To the beach
To the house I grew up in
To the crib I laid in when I was a baby
Everywhere.

Laura Tull (11)
Cookham Rise Primary School, Cookham

Jodie's Magic Box

(Based on 'Magic Box' by Kit Wright)

I will put in the box . . .
My rabbit as he jumps in the grass
And nibbles on weeds and stray plants
And my mirror
To make sure that I look OK for showing my face to the world.

I will put in the box . . .
My mum's aroma of perfume as it is going around the room
Coco, my chocolate-scented bunny
So I can smell chocolate all of the time.

I will put in the box . . .
Chocolate in my mouth which is just starting to melt
And fresh air to breathe in and out of my mouth.

I will put in the box . . .
My rabbit's soft ears and fur
And my mum's straw-like hair.

I will put in the box . . .
Birds tweeting in the trees in the morning and waking me up
And the wind blowing through me.

My box is fashioned with golden ribbons and silk buttons
And has a collar and a lead so that I can take it on walks.

I will take my box everywhere with me
And keep my box healthy by changing the hinges
And making sure that there are no scratches on it.
My box and I are together forever!

Jodie Macfarren (11)
Cookham Rise Primary School, Cookham

The Magic Box

(Based on 'Magic Box' by Kit Wright)

I will put in the box . . .
The feel of the soft sand of Spain,
The sun going down behind the palm tree,
The sound of sea hitting the rocks.

I will put in the box . . .
The smell of salty sea air,
The taste of sandy sandwiches,
The feel of rough coconut.

I will put in the box . . .
The sight of clear blue sea with tropical fish,
The sound of splashing sea water,
The smell of ice cream dripping down my finger.

I will put in my box . . .
The taste of chips, all salty and crunchy,
The feel of smooth shells,
The sound of seagulls swooping in the sky.

My box is made from smooth shells, driftwood and sand,
With sunsets on the lid and handles of string,
Its lock is made from a shark's tooth.

I shall keep my box through thick and thin,
Hot and cold,
I will keep it,
This box is mine forever.

Rebecca Brayne (11)
Cookham Rise Primary School, Cookham

My Pet

My pet
Swims in the river
And sleeps on land
At the moment
My pet
Has fur like a bear
Is cuter than a baby
He is quite rare
My pet
Also swims in the sea
He loves his home
And he belongs to me
My pet
Eats meat
He's got sharp teeth
And he's got his own seat
My pet
Doesn't fly
He doesn't rattle
And he hates veggie pies
My pet
Is very smart
And knows how to dance
He always plays darts
My pet
Is a rotter
He has a tail
And you should have noticed
He is an otter.

Naomi Rawlinson (11)
Cookham Rise Primary School, Cookham

Samantha's Magic Box

(Based on 'Magic Box' by Kit Wright)

I will put in the box . . .
The smell of sweet, freshly-baked bread,
The smell of melting chocolate floating up my nose,
And the feel of crispy leaves crunching under my feet.

I will put in the box . . .
The touch of freezing-cold ice cream touching my tooth,
The sound of a sweet nightingale
And the succulent taste of honey-glazed chicken.

I will put in my box . . .
The sight of my mum slapping her make-up on in the morning,
The silky-soft feeling of a newborn baby's skin
And the sound of fish fingers spitting in a pan.

I will put in the box . . .
The magnificent taste of my mum's roast chicken,
The sight of the sun slowly rising in the morning
And the sweet, lemony taste of pancakes.

My box is made of glittering stars of silver with pearl walls
That will hold in all my secrets.

I will treasure my box,
I will look after it forever,
I will hide it in a secret place that only I know
So no one will know its secrets.

Samantha Dance (11)
Cookham Rise Primary School, Cookham

My Magic Box!
(Based on 'Magic Box' by Kit Wright)

I will put in my box . . .
The sight of a dainty dolphin swimming gracefully,
Nightclub music
And a brilliant bacon butty.

I will put in my box . . .
A beautiful baby's smile
And the rustle of tissue paper,
Maybe even the smell of freshly baked bread.

I will put in my box . . .
An ice cliff I'm forced to climb,
Brussels sprouts I'm forced to eat
And the cracking of an egg I'm forced to hear.

I will put in my box . . .
Sweet-smelling, freshly cut grass
And the clip-clop of a foal's first steps,
A wet sponge with water oozing out.

I will put in my box . . .
The fizz of Coke tickling my tongue,
The end of a dog's ear, so soft, nuzzling my face
And the smell of a roast dinner so delicious.

The shells on my box shift around
Like they're playing a game,
The lock is made from octopus' suckers.

My box will take me far, far away to a deserted island,
Away from anyone,
Anyone that could steal my secrets.

Danielle Rickard (10)
Cookham Rise Primary School, Cookham

My Magic Box
(Based on 'Magic Box' by Kit Wright)

I will put in my box . . .
My rabbit's soft fur
The sound of my favourite band playing guitar
My tongue tasting chocolate

I will put in my box . . .
A million pounds
The smell of freshly cut grass
And a goal by Steven Gerrard

I will put in my box . . .
A frog jumping to a lily pad
A billion Yorkshire puddings
The lightest feather in the world

I will put in my box . . .
My guinea pig talking
The taste of prawn cocktail crisps
And my favourite movie

I will put in my box . . .
A rocket taking off into space
The brightest light
And a baby dinosaur

I shall ride my bike in my box
Over the world's biggest ramp
I shall take my bed
And sleep through the night.

Daniel John (11)
Cookham Rise Primary School, Cookham

Kane's Magic Box

(Based on 'Magic Box' by Kit Wright)

I will put in my box . . .
The smell of just-cooked cakes
Emerging from the oven,
Me drooling everywhere.

I will put in my box . . .
The sound of babies crying,
Laughing and playing
And messing around all night.

I will put in my box . . .
My friends,
Everyone I love
And everyone I care for.

I will put in my box . . .
My puppy staring
And always playing
Anywhere.

My box is made from gold and silver,
With love and care
And the lid holds secrets.

I shall share my box with the world,
I'll let everyone share my feelings
And spread happy feelings everywhere.

Kane Rose (11)
Cookham Rise Primary School, Cookham

My Magic Box

(Based on 'Magic Box' by Kit Wright)

I will put in my box . . .
The smell of my mum's cooking
The taste of ice cream melting in my mouth
The sight of rabbits hopping around in my garden.

I will put in my box . . .
The taste of rib and chips
The smell of hamsters
I like the sound of birds singing.

I will put in my box . . .
The sound of babies laughing
The soft touch of my rabbit's fur
And the taste of melting chocolate melting in my mouth.

In my black box is now gold and silver with stars inside it
And I will put on my padlock, a shell off the beach.

Sharmaine Hughes (11)
Cookham Rise Primary School, Cookham

Justin's Poem

An air flyer
A winged beast
A cloud passer
A fast air mover
A long machine
A speck as fast as a cannonball
A passenger carrier
A money-maker for humans like ourselves.

Justin James (11)
Cookham Rise Primary School, Cookham

The Magic Box

(Based on 'Magic Box' by Kit Wright)

I will put in my box . . .
The feel of a baby's palm
And the feeling of running my hands through the deep blue sea.

I will put in my box . . .
The sight of the big hand ticking round until the end of school
And to see a baby lamb take his first steps.

I will put in my box . . .
The sound of a bee buzzing around
And the sound of the wind blowing through the trees.

I will put in my box . . .
The smell of sizzling bacon,
The smell of melted chocolate and strawberries.

I will put in my box . . .
The taste of my favourite meal - macaroni cheese.

On the bottom of my box
I will put some legs so it can follow me wherever I go,
On top I will put a million magic sparkles to keep my luck.

I will use my box to keep all my deepest, darkest secrets in.

Rebecca Curley (11)
Cookham Rise Primary School, Cookham

Winter - Cinquain

Snowflakes
Drifting away
To a land not yet seen
Swaying, floating away, away
Snow drifts.

Charlotte Boulton (10)
Cookham Rise Primary School, Cookham

Clara's Magic Box!

(Based on 'Magic Box' by Kit Wright)

I will put in my box . . .
Lovely chocolate melting in my mouth,
Giraffes elegantly striding in the sunset,
The velvety fur of a sweet, newborn puppy.

I will put in my box . . .
The gorgeous lilies that sit in a vase,
The sound of waves crashing against the rocks,
A colourful fish gliding through the water.

I will put in my box . . .
The mountain peaks covered with snow,
The aroma of my mum's favourite perfume,
My dreams I know so well.

My box is made from wood,
And my name is engraved on it,
It is the best box ever.

I will dance like J-Lo on my box,
Whilst singing one of Usher's songs,
I will be the best,
Better than all the rest!

Clara Millar (11)
Cookham Rise Primary School, Cookham

In My Dream I Saw

A planet softly spin around over the stars.
I heard aliens zapping to each other
On the grey tarmac of a space centre.
In my dream I heard the shooting star glitter and rush in the black.
In my dream I saw a dog run like a cheetah under the sunset.

Mark Wilson (11)
Cookham Rise Primary School, Cookham

The Magic Box

(Based on 'Magic Box' by Kit Wright)

I will put in the box . . .
The dropkick that won the World Cup
And the penalty that missed, we were robbed!

I will put in the box . . .
The fans cheering and yelling
And my loud music playing.

I will put in the box . . .
The soft, gentle waves of the ocean
And the fluffiest pillow in the world.

I will put in the box . . .
The lovely smell of petrol
And a match that has just been blown out.

I will put in the box . . .
The soft bubbles of Coke on my tongue
And a glorious, juicy apple.

My box is made from solid titanium
And anyone who touches it gets burned
And the keyhole is a diamond.

I shall sleep in my box alongside all things I like.

Philip Hellmuth (11)
Cookham Rise Primary School, Cookham

Tongue Twister

Moany Maddie moaned at Mum
But if moany Maddie moaned at Mum
Why isn't moany Mum
Moaning at Maddie?

Maddison Heskett (9)
Drapers Mills CP School, Margate

My Body

I will start with my head
Because it's at the top
It's covered with a long,
Strawberry-blonde mop.

Then there are my eyes
That sparkle like stars
They are green like my brother's
Not blue like my mother's.

There's also my lips
All rosy and pink
And inside my head
Is my brain where I think.

I have two ears and also a nose
Two legs and two arms
Ten fingers, ten toes.

All of my parts
Are covered in skin
This keeps all of my organs
Nicely tucked in.

There are lots of things
As you can see
And all of these things
Make one little me!

Shannon Murray (9)
Drapers Mills CP School, Margate

Alliteration

Super Sarah Saw
Some Shiny Shells
Sparkling Slowly
When Sailing Salty Seas.

Sarah Galbraith (9)
Drapers Mills CP School, Margate

The Moon

The moon is like snow
It is as shiny as silk
As pretty as a crystal
The colour is milk

The moon is like an orange
Its shimmering light
Is just so bright
As pretty as a night

The moon is like a diamond
It is so bright
Ever so precious
Like the sunlight

The moon is like a ball
Just like a star
A glittering light
But ever so far

The moon is like a blur
Just like a kite
Makes it a beautiful sight
As shiny as a bike.

Charlotte Stratton (9)
Drapers Mills CP School, Margate

What Am I?

Thunder clapping,
Lightning flicking.
Clouds building,
Wind howling.
Electricity failing.
What am I?

Answer: The storm.

Shorab Dey (9)
Drapers Mills CP School, Margate

Birthdays

Birthdays, birthdays, what wonderful fun,
Let's all celebrate the birthday of the special one,
It's so great, you just can't wait,
Treats and sweets for everyone,
I like licking them with my tongue,
On the table treats, in the bowl sweets,
What would you have, treats or sweets?

Cards and presents from friends and family,
In your cards you might get money,
But I like presents more,
Tearing and ripping the presents
Are what makes birthdays good fun,
Boys get trousers, girls get flowers,
Girls like hearts, boys like tarts.

My birthday's in July, I don't know why,
On my birthday it's cool,
I get lots of cards and don't know where to put them,
Maybe in my bedroom,
Or maybe everywhere,
Birthdays are really fun.

Scarlett Preston (8)
Drapers Mills CP School, Margate

First Day Of School - Haiku

Don't know anyone
It's time to meet my teacher
It's really fun here!

Laura Myers (9)
Drapers Mills CP School, Margate

Bryn's Pockets

Bryn collects
Pieces of string
Insides of acorns
The little green things
Chewed-up bubblegum
Seeds and weeds
Treasures of the sea
And telephone leads

Bryn collects
Cogs and springs
Paper aeroplanes
The ones with wings
Banana skins
Nuts and bolts
Locks with no key
And packs of salt.

Bryn Llewellyn (9)
Drapers Mills CP School, Margate

Rabbit Burrow

There's a rabbit under the ground, *shush.*
If you're quiet it will come out, *shush.*
If you're noisy it will stay in, *shush.*

Lucy Bailey (9)
Drapers Mills CP School, Margate

A Kennings Poem

Blood-wanter
Night-walker
Human-scarer
Fiction-character
Teeth-long
Thirst-quencher
Seen-screamed
Wanted-not
Come-go
Sleeps-coffin
Cold-blooded
Skin-rough
Like a
Burglar creeping.
Who am I?

A vampire.

Charnice Maxted (8)
Drapers Mills CP School, Margate

Ruud Van Nistelrooy

Ruud van Nistelrooy can see the crowd roaring
He can see his teammates shouting for the ball
He can see the gigantic football stadium
He can see the massive pitch
Ruud van Nistelrooy can feel
He can feel electric while he scores a goal
He can feel the power of the ball
He can feel unhappy when he misses the ball.

Steven Taylor (10)
Drapers Mills CP School, Margate

The Writer Of This Poem Is . . .

(Based on 'The Writer of this Poem' by Roger McGough)

The writer of this poem
Is as bony as a skeleton
As bossy as my mum
As ugly as a rat

As smelly as a pig
As shy as a monkey
As slim as a person
As wild as a rhino

As white as a sheep
As light as a feather
As weak as a baby
As crunchy as an apple
As fast as a cheetah
As pretty as a princess.

Shannon Parker (9)
Drapers Mills CP School, Margate

The Writer Of This Poem Is . . .

(Based on 'The Writer of this Poem' by Roger McGough)

As naughty as a chimpanzee
As cheeky as a monkey
As fast as a cheetah
As scared as a mouse
As kind as a lady
As graceful as a swan
As great as a lion
It's me - I'm the writer of this poem!

Abigail Davies (9)
Drapers Mills CP School, Margate

Playtime

When the bell rings
We hear a big cheer
Lots of children running
The playground is near

Throw, jump, hopscotch played
Running children from 3rd grade
The whistle blows
The children stop
'Please, Miss, just one more hop!'

Grunting, groaning, stamping feet
Moaning back to their classroom seat
Muddy shoes, dripping wet
Isn't it lunchtime yet?

Katie Rogers (9)
Drapers Mills CP School, Margate

Kennings Poem

Blowing-whistle
People-passing
Balls-flying
Ball-in goal
People-sent off
Bad-tackler
Good-kicker
Children-cheering
Foot-breaker
Smile-breaker
Disappointed-players.
What am I?

Answer: Football game.

Gavin Ward (8)
Drapers Mills CP School, Margate

The Night's Eye

The moon rises,
Surprises the weary day
Like a sudden light.
Night-time.

The moon gleams,
Beams kindly light
Like a night light.
City freeze.

The moon sneaks,
Peaks through the dark cloud
Like a fast detective.
Alone at night.

The moon sleeps,
Creeps like a burglar
In the dark, dark night.
Alone by himself.

Anna Harris (9)
Drapers Mills CP School, Margate

The Sun

Sets beneath the clouds so grey
It pauses in the sky and lays
It shines like a burning ball of fire
It's never the stars
But placed much higher
It twinkles like the glittery star
Its place is set quite near to Mars
Its beams are light
As bulbs so bright
As it fades slowly and keeps quiet
Ready to go to bed
The moon disappears
The sun wakes up its sleepy head.

Anna Flood (9)
Drapers Mills CP School, Margate

What Am I?

Whistle blowing
Ball going to and fro
Ball scoring
Teams playing
People celebrating
Half-time
Kicking balls
Sweating
Subs
Free-kicks
Penalties
Corners
Offside
Yellow card
Red card
Teams
Injuries
Tackling
People watching
Won the match
Players playing
Sent off
Warning
Referee
Hard playing
Fun playing
Ball flying
Fans yelling
People booing
What am I?

Ashley Cole (9)
Drapers Mills CP School, Margate

Colours

Red like blood
All coming out of
You when you cut
Yourself.

Yellow like the
Sun, hot and
Fiery, burning all
Day long.

Pink like a
Flamingo doing
His dance in
The water.

Green like the
Grass swinging
Along with the
Wind.

Orange like the
Sand on the beach
In little grains like
Salt.

Purple like a
Plum, big and very
Juicy.

Blue like the
Sea where the
Seaweed and
Fish live.

Rachel Louise Buckley (10)
Drapers Mills CP School, Margate

Snowman

Snowman can see . . .
90 excited, naughty children throwing snowballs
Snowman can see
Children going down deep hills
Terrified, sledge super fast
And lots of cold snow.

Snowman can feel . . .
Sad and sometimes really mad
But most of all really happy
But sometimes really lonely.

Snowman can hear . . .
People screaming really loudly
Snowballs sloshing really hard
Naughty children crying
People's feet slashing in the snow.

Sandra Nightingale (9)
Drapers Mills CP School, Margate

My Family

My brother in the kitchen has slipped on some peas
And I had wobbly knees.
My mum dropped the coffee while Grandma ate toffee
And I got chased by the bees.

My auntie in tights,
My cousins having fights,
My uncle using paints,
Then they had to wait.

My nanny eating chips
And giving tips.
Nanny out all night
But she's alright.

Louise Dignam (10)
Drapers Mills CP School, Margate

Football

Whistle blowing
Goal scoring
People running
Kicking a ball
Teams
Half-time refreshments
Drinking water
Sweating bad
Injuries damage
Substitutes back up
Penalties excellent
Free kicks all right
Corners bending
Offside rubbish
Sent off
Fans screaming
Bad language
Yellow cards rising
Red cards rising rarely.

Daniel Galbraith (9)
Drapers Mills CP School, Margate

Fantastic Football

I see the crowds roaring at me,
Shouting my name with glee.
The manager is supporting me
With the World Cup in front of me.
I feel so excited when I score,
So excited I jump up and down on the floor.
At the end of the match I am really tired,
Aching bones, but at least I'm admired.

Daniella Rossiter (10)
Drapers Mills CP School, Margate

Humour In My Family

My mum can see
My dad dripping with paint
He must have dropped
Paint on his head.
Humour in my family.
My nanny can see
My great granny
Slipping over spaghetti.
Humour in my family.
My auntie can see
My mum sitting down
And finds her on the ground.
Humour in my family.
My cousin Ben
Having fun
Accidentally dropped his bun.
Humour in my family.
I can see
The people in my family.

Victoria Reason (9)
Drapers Mills CP School, Margate

Star Wars

S tars shining in the sky.
T he spaceships blasting baddies.
A ttack of the Clones.
R ight through their bones.

W ar has started with baddies.
A ll is done, the battle is won.
R un off pesky Clones.
S kywalker will slash your bones.

Rees Peterson (10)
Drapers Mills CP School, Margate

Pluto

I am a planet of anger so deep,
But it cannot be seen,
For I am engulfed with a long, dreamy sleep,
I shall never be discovered,
Life is too far from me.

But you shall find me very, very soon,
And then you shall see,
That I'm but a small ball of ice,
Then I'll be happy,
Then I'll be nice.

For you have bothered to look,
Then (like all the other planets),
I shall be recorded in more than one book,
I shall be famous just like Earth,
And then the new birth
Of Pluto begins.

Sam Gilbert (11)
East Preston Junior School, East Preston

Red

Red is the colour of gory blood
Also the colour of true love.
The colour of your heart
Not the colour of your veins.
It's the colour of your wounds
When you've got some pains.
Red is the colour of anger
When you feel ready to destroy.
It's the colour of the heart of fire
As well as your lover's desire.

Brett Pine (10)
East Preston Junior School, East Preston

The Lonely Planet

As I sit here alone I'm as cold as ice,
Alone, on my own, I am always frozen.

Asteroids and comets tend to visit,
Alone, on my own, I have no companions.

My skin is cold as I'm far from the sun,
Alone, on my own, I am always cold.

As the days pass I watch stars shoot by,
Alone, on my own, I see flickers of light.

Sometimes I feel I've disappeared altogether,
Alone, on my own, I will soon die out.

I am forever Pluto!

Victoria Balsdon (11)
East Preston Junior School, East Preston

Space

There's space around us everywhere,
Even when it's daytime stars are still there.
Mercury is a small planet like a brown ball,
Venus is next and is hottest of all.
Earth is our planet with life, it's our home,
The fourth planet Mars is where Martians roam!
Jupiter is the biggest gassy ball,
Saturn has lots of rings and is my favourite of all.
The seventh planet, Uranus, green gasses shining bright,
Neptune is next and can be seen in the night.
Lonely Pluto is the furthest away,
These are our planets in the Milky Way.

Eden Smith (11)
East Preston Junior School, East Preston

Jupiter

As my body draws fierce comets with burning fury towards me,
I flatter them with magnificent beauty,
And they slow down and change course.

My colossal but dying eyes refuse to look towards other planets,
For they do not know the pain that grows inside me.
The horde of comets that crash into my core every second,
My only friends are my moons.

The never-ending blackness surrounds me, laughs at me
And calls me names,
Sadness swallows me up.

As one last comet crashes into my gassy surface
And reaches my core,
With my flattering technique failed, I call out to my moons,
And after years of suffering, finally die.

Ben Cripps (11)
East Preston Junior School, East Preston

Arrow

Air cutter
Swift flyer
Feather tail
Heart breaker
Armour piercer
Pain pricker
Sky reacher
Skin piercer.

Alastair Finlinson & Luke Bridger (11)
East Preston Junior School, East Preston

Aliens

Do they really exist
Or is it all myth?
These out of space
Creatures.

With their one middle eye,
Their dangly limbs,
And their horrible slime-trail they leave behind.

Who has really seen them?
Who has really been slimed by them?
Have you?

To me they are all make-believe,
Little children they deceive,
To keep them in the their beds at night,
Threatened by fear and the chance of a fright!

Lauren Andrews (11)
East Preston Junior School, East Preston

Poor Pluto

Baby of the universe, cold and alone,
Daddy Jupiter so far away from me.
My silk, cold coat gives me a chill,
I try to get it off but it just won't budge.

Dusty and miserable, down and gloomy,
I sit here freezing whilst also alone,
My big brother Neptune,
I hardly ever see, back in darkness.

Comets and asteroids annoying me,
Banging and crashing into poor me.
I am so cold up here,
Yes, I am poor Pluto!

Maddie Moore (10)
East Preston Junior School, East Preston

Mercury's Warrior Within

Having the sun as your neighbour,
You take the heat as a challenge.
Your rock-hard skin,
Scarred all over.
But still you go on,
Duelling for your friends.
Venus is your ally,
Reinforcements just in case,
Defending Earth from its fatal doom.
Your eyes fixed on your nemesis,
Never looking back to the days before man.
Without you by our side,
We will certainly fall,
But we are confident that won't happen.
After centuries of experience,
The battle will go on,
For many years to come.
Please stay with us,
We need you.

Eddie Blandamer (11)
East Preston Junior School, East Preston

Star

Pitch
Then suddenly
A twinkle, brighter, brighter
A star luminescent with pride
Flitters and glitters, gliding smoothly through
The air so bright, so fiery
But not for long
For the star ends
Its beautiful
Song.

Anastasia Perysinakis (8)
East Preston Junior School, East Preston

Pluto's Life Story

The warmth of the sun only just reaches me
I am always cold.

The size of the others makes me feel like a toddler,
I am always tiny.

Asteroids and comets are my only companions,
I am always lonely.

The breath that I breathe just forms small ice drops,
I am always frozen.

Each time that I cry no one hears me,
I am always sad.

The jokes that I tell just echo around me,
I am always dull.

Hardly seeing anyone, even Neptune, just sitting up here,
I am always alone.

My jealousy of Mercury is almost overwhelming,
I am always chilled.

As I am the youngest, I have to just stay here,
I am always jobless.

I am freezing and tiny, chilled and alone,
I am always Pluto.

Emma Withers (11)
East Preston Junior School, East Preston

Poor Neptune

I am a shivering, frozen planet,
Nobody loves me,
And I'm feeling kind of down.
My ice-cold rings surround me,
And wave about to get attention,
But no one ever sees me.
My only friend is my ring,
But here I am curled up,
Curled up in a ball of ice.
My body so cold I can't believe my eyes.
I have never been visited by another planet,
Only ever passed me in their orbit,
Which brings me right down the line.
I do have feelings,
I do have courage,
But I'm so far down,
I'm just no one.

Jamie Worsa (11)
East Preston Junior School, East Preston

Moon + Mars = Space!

Out there is the moon,
I hope I'll get there soon.
It is my desire to fly,
Into the sky and land upon the moon.

There is a planet called Mars,
It is not as far as the stars.
It is said the planet is red,
Unlike chocolate bars.

Chris Moore (11)
East Preston Junior School, East Preston

The Vulture

They say I'm ugly with my unusual look,
But I never once have to even cook.
They think I am lazy just flying around,
Just sitting and watching the world go around.
A lioness is chasing, she's running like mad,
She's close to her prey, a kill - I'll be glad.
The fatal bite to the neck and the deer is dead,
She carries it to her cubs,
And soon they'll be fed.
The feast begins under a camel thorn tree,
In the distance hyenas gather, I can see.
The lions finish, their banquet is done,
My wait was worth it, my turn has come.
I have to be quick because others are near,
I take what I can of the succulent deer.

Aisha Cove (8)
East Preston Junior School, East Preston

Jumba Kenya

The safari guide said to me,
'Jump in the jeep and let's see what we can see.'
Chimpanzees swimming through the trees,
Others are sitting picking each other's fleas.
Elephants big and grey,
Springboks running wild and free.
Lions chasing their prey hoping for a delicious tea,
Hippos swimming in the mud, oh what fun,
Cooling down from the sun.
The sun is setting bright and red,
The safari guide said, 'It's time for bed.'

Harry Forrest (9)
East Preston Junior School, East Preston

The Story Of Jim Who Would Not Swim

Jim was a happy chap,
He swam round from back to back,
Everyone yelled and cheered,
But still everyone called him weird.
He always did as he was told,
And never let his pool get cold.
But one day - one cold day,
He shouted, 'I won't go swimming today!
Oh don't fill the pool today!
I *won't* go swimming today!'

Next day comes, oh poor Jim,
He still decides he doesn't want to swim.
He starts to get very big,
He's almost as big as a pig.
He shouted, 'I won't go swimming today!
Oh don't fill the pool today!
I *won't* go swimming today!'

The third day comes, oh what a sin!
The pool is full and he still won't jump in.
Jim's friends start to say, 'Oh just jump in today!'
Jim just says, 'Oh go away!
Don't ever get in my way!'
He shouted, 'I won't go swimming today!
Oh don't fill the pool today!
I *won't* go swimming today!'

Look at him now the fourth day's come!
He now weighs at least a ton.
He spends all his time in bed,
And on the fifth day he was - dead!

Leah Childs (9)
East Preston Junior School, East Preston

Predator

Heat seeker
Skull collector
Heart ripper
Body skinner
Human reaper
Man's nightmare
Spear wielder
Alien killer
Invisible hunter
Power seeker
Civilisation ruler
Holy fighter
Death bringer
Life taker
Acid marker
Shoulder gunner
Widow maker
Technology inventor
Bone breaker
Hangman player
Blade thrower
Armour piercer
Spear master
Honourable warrior
Spaceship flyer
War champion.

Gary Burger (11)
East Preston Junior School, East Preston

The Animals Of Kenya

I was thinking of all the animals in Kenya that I like best.
The biggest and the hairiest
Is a gorilla when he beats his chest.

Another of which I am fond
Is the hippo in a pond.
But the one that appeals to me
Is the monkey in his tree.

I used to like the lion
Until he ate my cousin Brian.
But that's nothing to the snake
That swallowed my uncle Jake!

Connor Mott (9)
East Preston Junior School, East Preston

Red And Black

Red, the colour of dripping blood
The colour of angry men
The colour of true love
Also the colour of shame and disappointment
Red, the colour of destruction
When it comes to black I hide in fear
Black is the colour of the dark side
It is the colour of a pitch-black night
So red and black together
Now you know about that forever.

Bobby Wiffen (9)
East Preston Junior School, East Preston

Jack-In-The-Box

                        !
                        G
                        N
                        I
Wind it, wind it, wind it . . . P
My name is Jack and I'm on a s-p-r-i-n-g
I bounce up here and over there
Down comes the lid, it's just not fair
Back I go - back where I started
For once again I've been outsmarted!

Alice Leadbeatter (10)
East Preston Junior School, East Preston

Purple

Purple is the colour of an angry sky.
It's the happy version of black.
You can hear it when you walk through a graveyard at night.
Is it a colour of a memory you wouldn't forget?
Purple's the colour of expensive riches!
It's the last colour of the mourning trail.
But most of all purple is the colour of the end of the world . . .

Mark Leyton (10)
East Preston Junior School, East Preston

Black

Black is the outline of a haunted house,
You can hear it in the cry of a helpless person.
It's the colour of your follower.
Black is the cast of a starless sky at night.
It's the colour of a memory you would rather forget.
You can feel it when the wind rustles against your face at night.
That's what black is.

Harvey Woods (10)
East Preston Junior School, East Preston

Teachers

Teachers can be mean
They usually aren't green

Teachers are like spies
They can see who's talking with the blink of an eye

Teachers are usually old
They are always bold

In a flash
They're at a bash

Look at the plane in the sky
Look out, Miss is watching us with her watchful eye

It's nearly lunchtime
Yuck! I can see the teacher's spine!

Joseph Kerney (7)
Foxborough Primary School, Slough

Through That Door A Royal Palace

Through that door
Live the king and the queen
Their daughter the princess
Has to be seen!
Her beauty is famous
Throughout the land
A handsome prince
Has asked for her hand
The daughter agreed
There'll be a huge ball
Morning till midnight
Music will fill the hall.

Manisha Kumar (9)
Foxborough Primary School, Slough

The Old King Of Windsor Castle

The old king of Windsor castle,
He received a special parcel,
And never did you hear such a groany, moany moan.
'Open this, open that!
I want my pussycat!'

The old king of Windsor castle,
He had an enormous parcel,
And never did you hear such a groany, moany moan.
'I want this, I want that!
I want my pussycat!'

The old king of Windsor castle,
He had a big parcel,
And never did you hear such a groany, moany moan.
'I want this, I want that!
I want my pussycat,
And that is that!'

Lucy Cooper (10)
Foxborough Primary School, Slough

Clock

I am a ticker
I wake my owner
I shake my body
I am a number shiner
I am a morning waker
I am a lunchtime teller
I am a c . . . c . . . c . . . clock.

Stacey Edwards (9)
Foxborough Primary School, Slough

My Alphabet Poem

A is for Abbie who is always arguing.
B is for Brandon who is always bouncing.
C is for Charlotte who is always chattering.
D is for Danielle who is always daring.
E is for Eddie who is always eating.
F is for Frankie who is always funny.
G is for Georgina who is always giggling.
H is for Hannah who is always doing her homework.
I is for Ivy who is always coming out with ideas.
J is for Jake who is always jumping.
K is for Kelly who acts like kangaroo.
L is for Luke who hates Laura,
M is for Michelle who acts like a mum.
N is for Natasha whose best friend is Natalie.
O is for Ozzie who looks like an octopus.
P is for Poppy who loves picking poppies.
Q is for Queenie who acts like a queen.
R is for Roy who loves rock 'n' roll.
S is for Sophie who eats lots of sweets.
T is for Tyler who has a kitten called Twinkle.
U is for Una who hates her nickname 'U'.
V is for Vicky, her mum calls her Victoria.
W is for Wendy, her last name is Webb.
X is for X-ray lady, she works with the X-ray man.
Y is for Yasmin who never says *yuck!*
Z is for Zenum, she knows her alphabet A to Z.

Chloe Bowler
Foxborough Primary School, Slough

The Sound Collector

(Based on 'The Sound Collector' by Roger McGough)

'A stranger called this morning
Dressed all in black and grey
Put every sound into a bag
And carried them away'

The shouting of the kids
The banging of the drawers
The scratching of the board pens
The slamming of the doors

The creaking of the door
The zipping of the pencil case
The humming of the lights
The tying of the lace

The flicking of the pages
The scratching of the pen
The laughing of the children
They're counting one to ten

'A stranger called this morning
He didn't leave his name
Left us only in silence
Life will never be the same'.

Jade Scammell (8)
Foxborough Primary School, Slough

Little Bo Peep

There once was a girl
Called Little Bo Peep
Her job was to look
After all her sheep

One fine day
She put on her coat
Grabbed her crook
But she had a sore throat

She called and called
But the sheep didn't come
So she started to search,
'These sheep are so dumb.'

She looked in the field
She looked in the barn
And there they all were
They'd come to no harm

She was so, so pleased
That her sheep were back
She put down her crook
Hung her coat on the rack.

Bethany Payne   (9)
Foxborough Primary School, Slough

Summer Days

Summer days are here to stay
Lots of water fights for you and me
Time to sit in the sun with Mum
Singing birds in the trees and buzzy bees

Making sandcastles on the beach
Licking sticky lemon lollies
Mum eating strawberries and cream
Little girls play with dollies

Waves tickling my toes and feet
Mum calling me, it's time to go
'No, just bit longer please,' I say
But Mum says, We'll come back
Another day!'

Hurriyyah Wasim (9)
Foxborough Primary School, Slough

The Slow Worm

The slow worm slithers through grass
Eating insects on its way.

When night comes
Asleep it will lay until the next day.

His scaly body is really smooth
A slow worm is always on the move.

The slow worm wraps tightly around my fingers
Like a snake.

He collects grass
And a great home he will make.

Luke Austin (10)
Foxborough Primary School, Slough

Riddle

I am
Black or white,
Ginger or brown,
And multicoloured,
Smaller than an elephant,
But bigger than an ant,
Water-drinker,
Fur-licker,
Mouse-catcher,
Thin tail,
Pointy ears,
Fish-snatcher,
Fur coat.

I am a . . .
Cat!

Kewita Bassi
Foxborough Primary School, Slough

Butterfly, Butterfly

It's as soft as velvet.
It's as gentle as a baby.

It's as calm as a picture.
It's as pretty as pink.

The eyes are as blue as the sky.
The eyes are as colourful as the rainbow.

The butterfly isn't nearly as pretty as my *mum!*

Abbie Burden (9)
Foxborough Primary School, Slough

The Heart

The heart, the heart is full of love
The heart, the heart is like a dove
The heart, the heart is ruby red.

My heart belongs to
My friends and family
My heart's love will
Never end.

The heart, the heart is
So precious to me
The heart, the heart
Help me be.

The heart, the heart is a
Piece of me
My heart's destiny is
For my true love.

Charlotte Quelch (10)
Foxborough Primary School, Slough

A Magic Horse

Through that door
I see a big, green field
With lots of horses
And a stable you can build
With water and food
The food is hay
I can see a horse
Going *neigh! Neigh! Neigh!*

Charlotte Woods (9)
Foxborough Primary School, Slough

Witches Song

(Inspired by 'Macbeth')

Double, double toil, trouble
Fire burn and cauldron bubble
Chopped up worms
With frogs' spawns
A dead hand
With mouldy sand

A black spider with a tiger
And a dead cat with
A rat that is flat

A dead fish
With a dish
Some dead mice with a spice.

Brandon Cottrell
Foxborough Primary School, Slough

Playing Children

Children playing, having fun,
Crunching leaves as they run.

Jumping in puddles, feeding the ducks,
Dressing up like a million bucks.

Munching their tea, munch and crunch,
Scoffing bananas in a bunch.

Catching frogs, they leap and jump,
Eating custard, spitting lumps.

Night has come, their mums said,
'Time for you to go to bed.'

Munayyat Abdallah (10)
Foxborough Primary School, Slough

Witch's Spell

(Inspired by 'Macbeth')

Double, double toil and trouble,
Fire burn and cauldron bubble.
Robin's wing not to sing,
And a touch of a wasp's sting.
Dragon's tooth, dragon's brain,
Freshly delivered from Spain.

Fish tails, bird's bones,
Mixed together with stones.
Dog's tail, frog's legs,
Mixed up with some croc eggs.

Double, double toil and trouble,
Fire burn and cauldron bubble.
Cool it down with whale eyes,
Mixed together with green flies.

Bradley Daw (9)
Foxborough Primary School, Slough

Autumn Days

A utumn days when people get cold
U nder and over the leaves swirl while they cartwheel down
T o the brown earth below
U ncontrollable leaves going madly insane
M any leaves have gone crunchy
N uts and berries have grown sweet and juicy

D edicated to berries the squirrel runs
A s lively as a tiger
Y ellow leaves float around
S oaring through the air.

Lauren Phillips (8)
Foxborough Primary School, Slough

Double Trouble

(Inspired by 'Macbeth')

Double, double toil and trouble!
Fire burn and cauldron bubble
A speck of dust
The frog eyes going bust
Big juicy frogs' legs
All hanging on pegs

Lizard eyes mashed with dung
All wrapped up in a lung
Big piles of yellow snot
Go well in a pot

Tongues of snakes in a jar
Reed of a lake smashed up by a bar
Cool it down with worm blood
Make sure you add the mud!

Bradley McCarten (9)
Foxborough Primary School, Slough

Riddle

I am
A tall animal,
With a very long neck,
Lots of yellow and brown patches,
I am the tallest of all the mammals,
I eat leaves from the top of the tree,
I have 4 legs and a tail.
What am I?
Answer: A giraffe!

Debbie Seagrove
Foxborough Primary School, Slough

Tiger

I am
A brilliant bite killer
A growl talker
A great stalker
A brilliant sensor
A brilliant hunter
A brilliant eater
A brilliant furry animal
A great animal killer
A great hunter
A great animal that hunts for meat
A t . . . t . . . tiger.

Stephen Sissons (9)
Foxborough Primary School, Slough

Shape Poem

Angels
Singing
Loudly, waking
Baby Jesus
Mary and Joseph
Sing a lullaby to help
Baby Jesus to sleep
'Hush
Hush
My little
Baby son.'

Veronica Nicholls (9)
Foxborough Primary School, Slough

Untitled

If I were a star on a bright night
I would sparkle and twinkle.
I would brighten up the dark park.
I would dazzle with my beauty.
I would dance with you in the sky.

If I were a star on a stormy night
I would fight with the clouds.
I would leave the sky dark.
I would run away with the moon.

Hannah Brown (8)
Foxborough Primary School, Slough

School!

School, school, it is so boring,
At the end of the day we're snoring.

The classroom stinks of smelly sweat,
A geeky boy ends up soaking wet.

The playground is a skiing pad,
In the winter it is fab.

Teachers always talk a lot,
Until they boil and lose the plot.

Children, children are the best,
They always lay back and have a rest.

Jessica Peters (9)
Georgian Gardens CP School, Rustington

Teddy

This is my teddy
With only one eye
He never speaks, he's very shy.

This is my teddy
All cuddly and soft
I'll never leave him in the loft.

This is my teddy
I've had him for a while
I think it's ever since I could smile.

This is my teddy
He's the best
He could beat yours, it wouldn't be a test.

Elliot Horne (10)
Georgian Gardens CP School, Rustington

End Of Summer Term

Right, now class has begun,
What on Earth are you doing, son?

Chloe, enough with picking your nose,
Lydia, please put back the hose.

Jamie, put that fag away,
Sorry, Luke dear, what did you say?

Right, I've had enough,
Jenny dear, do up your cuff.

Oh thank goodness your mums are here,
Peace and quiet until next year.

Rhiannon Limmer (10)
Georgian Gardens CP School, Rustington

Pink Bunny

This is my bunny
All rough and worn
He's like a cute kitten
Lying on the lawn.

This is my bunny
He sleeps in my bed
Sometimes I chuck him
Over my head.

This is my bunny
He's ugly but warm
Really, he's just right.

Kayleigh Mengham (10)
Georgian Gardens CP School, Rustington

Spring

Here comes spring eager to begin,
Out come the birds starting to sing.

A little bit of rain and maybe some sun,
Out pop the children having lots of fun.

In go the grey clouds, out come the white,
People's faces changing from miserable to bright.

Everyone enjoys birds starting to sing,
Here comes spring eager to begin.

Emilia Ceccarelli (10)
Georgian Gardens CP School, Rustington

Pets

Dogs and puppies are lots of fun,
They always like to run in the sun.

Hamsters are so fluffy and cute,
They're about the size of a boot.

Fish just like to swim around,
Without making lots of sound.

Birds over here, birds over there,
Wherever you look, they're everywhere.

Animals think they are the best,
Well, they are better than the rest.

Jade Mills (10)
Georgian Gardens CP School, Rustington

Spring

Birds awaking, rabbits making
Trouble already in the spring sun.

Sun is shining, birds are finding
Places to rest in the spring sun.

Daffodils growing, lawns need mowing
So kids say in the spring sun.

Spring sheep breeding, chickens need feeding
Seed and corn in the spring sun.

Victoria Sopp (10)
Georgian Gardens CP School, Rustington

Dyslexia

Anger, frustration looking at the page,
Desire inside me changing to rage,
I want to do it, but I can't
My brain says, 'No, no you shan't!'

Hard, impossible - I don't care,
Words are flying everywhere.
I really want to be a reading buddy
But I never will be, however hard I study.

I'm like a normal person on the outside
But my mixed up brain is twisted and tied.
I'm happy because my legs are long
And when I'm scoring goals they are really strong.

'Hooray!' shouts the crowd
And I am really proud.
It doesn't matter that I can't read
Because, at this moment, there is no need.

Greg Trencher (11)
Georgian Gardens CP School, Rustington

Egg

Bald egg, bald egg, over there
What's it like to have no hair?

Is it nice or is it bad?
What's it like to be really sad?

Is it hell to have a shell
Or is it like a giant bell?

Is it cold when you're sold
When you're barely one month old?

Nick Sopp (10)
Georgian Gardens CP School, Rustington

The One And Lonely

There is a beach hut perched high upon a cliff
Towering above the rest.
My mother used to say that the hut was made for guests.
I turned to face her and said,
'How can this marvellous thing go to waste?'
And to this day everyone forgot about the beach.

I woke one night with a quiver down my spine.
I clambered out of my bed and followed a white line.
I didn't know what I was doing
But I struggled outside and started stumbling towards the hut.
The neighbours watching started to tut.
I saw the birds in a flock drifting into the mist.
I saw the boats in the docks bobbing gently up and down.

I listened carefully to the rippling sea
And saw a wonderful, shining key.
'Where are you? Where are you?' I heard someone call.
'I'm here, I'm here,' as I started to fall.

I could feel warmness bubbling inside me
And coldness whisping as the air surrounded me.
'I'm lonely,' I called. 'I'm lonely.'

Zoë Adams (11)
Georgian Gardens CP School, Rustington

Spring

Spring floats in as birds start to sing,
Rabbits hop in the dewy grass,
Gusty winds fade away,
More children go out to play,
April showers fall down,
Sometimes they even flood the town.

Annabel Smith (10)
Georgian Gardens CP School, Rustington

Pencil

I know a pencil full of lead,
It gives me the thoughts within my head.
It moves across the paper, nice and smooth,
And lets my hand freely move.
I know a pencil nice and fat,
It gives me ideas about a fat cat.
I write about a famous band,
As well as about the sea and the sand.
My fat pencil's grey and old,
It makes my work look nice and bold.
My pencils go where'er I go,
Whether I go up or come down low.
My last pencil was the third,
After the one with the bird.
My last pencil is fading away,
Because I use it every day.

Nicole Pearce (11)
Georgian Gardens CP School, Rustington

Rubbish

I'm rubbish at poems,
I can't do a thing.
The paper I write on,
Ends up in the bin.
Writing poems I just don't know how,
So I can't be bothered to do this one now.
I really can't think of anything worse,
Than writing a stupid poetry verse.

Louis Valentine (10)
Georgian Gardens CP School, Rustington

My Teddy

This is my teddy, orange and black,
He is old,
And lives in a sack.

This is my teddy, soft and furry,
Fur spiked out,
And looks like curry.

This is my teddy, cute and cuddly,
He is lucky,
And is so lovely.

Ben West (10)
Georgian Gardens CP School, Rustington

Parents

Parents, parents are so boring,
When they sleep they're always snoring.

My dad's woolly jumper has to go,
And he really needs to shave his toes.

My mum's clothes are horrid and old,
They smell like rotten, smelly mould.

Right, that's it, I've had enough,
I'm moving out of here - that's tough.

Danielle Brown (10)
Georgian Gardens CP School, Rustington

Kids

Kids, kids are the best
In the winter they wear a vest

When it comes to the end of the day
I always shout, *'Hip hip hooray!'*

When the school bell does ring
Everyone just gives a sing

If we kids cause such a fuss
Why do you go on having us?

Harriet Mayhead (10)
Georgian Gardens CP School, Rustington

Ghost House

This is the scream
That comes from the train
When we see the face
That follows the hand
That shakes the chain
That rattles the train
That rumbles the floor
As it goes through the door
To the ghost house.

Antonia Lunn (11)
Georgian Gardens CP School, Rustington

Seashore

The seashore splashes,
It splashes all around,
The seashore is so calm,
And it makes a lovely sound.

The seagulls fly over,
They are really, really soft,
They have a good sense of direction,
And would never get lost.

And then again the seashore,
Where everything is calm,
Everything is restful,
At the seashore there is no harm.

Samah Hussain (8)
Holyport CE Primary School, Holyport

Swimming

Swimming is the thing for me
It's splashing, crashing, *miraculous*
I go swimming four times a week
Swimming races make me *nervous*
It is difficult sometimes
Even though it is so *glorious*
Swimming classes are so fun
But I am very fast and *furious*
I am in Junior B right now
And my friends they are *hilarious*
They say that I am brill at it
Because I am a *genius.*

Philippa Bailey (10)
Holyport CE Primary School, Holyport

My Dog Bruno!

My dog Bruno
He jumps and bumps around a lot!
He can run! He takes all the crumbs!
He is very cute and very hairy
But very scary when he barks!
But he is scared of the dark!
But I don't care because we are just a pair
And he is still the best dog in the world to me!
My dog Bruno!

Jade Hill (8)
Holyport CE Primary School, Holyport

Where You Hide

Where you hide
The shadow dances like a forgotten spirit.

Where you hide
The sharp brambles with outstretched thorns
Like sharpened fingernails.

Where you hide
Dancing toadstools in the moonlight.

Where you hide
Crouching behind the brambles a hidden flash of lightning.

Where you hide
Beside the prickly corn stalks beneath the dust.

Where you hide
Deep within sniggering bushes, a rabbits' nest.

Jake Sellwood (11)
Kingsclere CE Primary School, Kingsclere

Weather

Sunshine.
Light staring face to face
Eye to eye at me
As it burns my face until it's crumbly
Fades away behind ghosts.

Fog.
A cold blanket
Covering everyone with its spells.

Frost.
Danger breathing down my back
As it freezes up my spine.

Rain.
Spitting water as I try to get away from it.
It gets you drenched.

Snow.
Icy diamonds dancing in the air as I try to catch them,
But they disappear in seconds.

Hail.
Spitting ice drops down upon me
As I quickly get away into warm shelter.

Thunder.
Eye-blinding duvet of warmth
Surrounding me as I run.

Lightning.
Jumping up and down with static shocks
Sparking in my spiky hair.

Rupert Broad (10)
Kingsclere CE Primary School, Kingsclere

Wicked Witches Works

(Inspired by 'Macbeth')

Bubble, bubble, boil and brew,
Fire glazes and cauldron stew,
Tail of an Atlantic rat,
In the mixture of gooey fat,
Ear of fish and fin of frog,
Rhino's egg and mud from bog.

Bat stomach and smell of sea,
Coffee beans and bags of tea,
For a spell of power brew,
Like a hell-broth boiling of stew.

Bubble, bubble, boil and brew,
Fire glazes and cauldron stew,
Finish it off with this chant,
Reggle, dangle, doodle grant.

Hannah Martin & Marianne Borzoni (10)
Kingsclere CE Primary School, Kingsclere

Where You Hide

Where you hide
A wooden shack on a riverbank
Deep within a forgotten wood.

Where you hide
A hidden corner of a hay barn
As the rats scurry around their homes.

Where you hide
A hidden temple
In a lost world.

Jonathan Cotter (10)
Kingsclere CE Primary School, Kingsclere

Dear Mrs Ridler

(Inspired by 'Dear Mum' by Brian Patten)

While you were out
A book flew off the shelf
And broke the new watch you bought
Last Sunday morning.
And somehow the board rubber rubbed off all the instructions.
Suddenly, without walking past,
The coats they fell off their hangers
And made a big pile on the floor.
I don't think we'll ever work out
How the computer overheated (while it was off).
Without touching the CD player
The peaceful, calm music turned into loud rock and pop music.
Independently, the window opened
And all the paper flew off the board.
Mysteriously, while I was sitting the other side of the room
The windows started wobbling and smashed to the ground.
I didn't spill your tea again so I don't know how it spilt everywhere.
Knowing you would go round the twist
We have gone over to Mrs McGeorge's classroom till after lunch.

Hannah Bright & Pippa Allwood (10)
Kingsclere CE Primary School, Kingsclere

The Register

(In the style of 'The Register' by Michael Rosen)

Right, class, register time.
Jeffery, it doesn't matter the clock is half a minute slower than
your watch.
Robert, leave the worms alone.
No, they're not jelly worms.
No, they're not.
Now, has anyone seen the register?
Jeffery, leave the clock alone.
Sarah, don't kick David.
I'm sure he doesn't like it.
David, do you?
No, stop it then, Sarah.
Oh hello, Mr Brush.
What's that?
Ah, class, if Mr Brush finds any more muddy footprints outside the
classroom he'll make you clean them up yourselves.
What's that, Robert?
You feel sick?
You didn't eat a worm, did you?
Oh no, you did! You better go down to the nurse's office immediately.
Now, where's the . . .
Samantha, don't take the fish out of their tank.
Now, who's seen the register?
I said, *who's seen the register?*

Ben Rampton & Nicholas Jenkins (10)
Kingsclere CE Primary School, Kingsclere

Dear Mrs McGeorge

(Inspired by 'Dear Mum' by Brian Patten)

While you were out,
A mug of coffee smashed over the new plasma TV
Causing it to blow up,

Your special marking that took ages to do
Took a test flight into the shredder,

Not to mention the new pencils you got
Being attacked by giant, man-eating ants,

Also a family of piranhas seem to have a hunger for knowledge
And digested your school reports,

Oh and I was forgetting
Your old budgie tried to act 'The Great Escape'
And set off the fire alarm,

So knowing you're going to blast-off
We've all gone home with a nasty cough!

George Caren & Imogen Brown (11)
Kingsclere CE Primary School, Kingsclere

Night

The mist circling the summit of the towering skyscrapers,
The city streets as quiet as a mouse,
Shadows lurking in the petrifying alleys,
Rats hurriedly scurry out of the revolting sewer drains,
Cats disturbingly whine,
The old, abandoned graveyards, so terrifying,
You frantically run past.
When all is asleep, as silent as the dead,
The monsters come out to play and go when dawn comes . . .

Louise Knapp (10)
Leigh Primary School, Tonbridge

The Magic Box

(Based by 'Magic Box' by Kit Wright)

I will put in the box . . .
The golden glint of sunlight captured on the wing
            of a super sonic aircraft,
The sweet scent of newly fried pancakes on a sunny Easter morning,
The swift flick of an ancient page in a leather-bound classic.

I will put in the box . . .
The swift sweep of a waterfall of shining chestnut hair,
A scoop of scarlet sunset disappearing on the emerald horizon,
The stylish aroma of perfume on the elegant neck
            of a beautiful woman.

I will put in the box . . .
The tender love of a mild mother and a newborn child,
The touch of a great elephant, stroking its tiny baby,
The hollow moan of a peaceful blue whale on a moonlit evening.

I will put in the box . . .
A cup of amber liquid from an erupting volcano, far-off in the East,
The strong scent of brewing wine that haunts a grape vineyard,
An oak tree growing cocoa beans and a cocoa tree growing acorns.

My box is fashioned out of the scarred wood of the enormous oak,
That was seeded when time began.
With stardust on the lid, planets in the corners and spiderwebs
            lining the inside.
Its hinges are Zeus bent lightning bolts.

I shall fly in my box,
Over many high mountains and sleeping oceans,
Then land on a shining star
And dance with the delicate fairies.

Ellie Warr (11)
Leigh Primary School, Tonbridge

The Magic Box

(Based by 'Magic Box' by Kit Wright)

I will put in my magic box . . .
The tender love of a tiny tot,
The swish of a soft swift tea,
The magical light from midnight stars.

I will put in my box . . .
A grass green frog leaping from stone to stone,
A rocking horse prancing over every jump,
The dew clinging to silky spiderwebs in the early morning.

I will put in my box . . .
Three emerald-green secrets,
The last song of a seagull,
The first giggle of a baby girl.

My box is fashioned from ice to silver,
The planets on the lid and wishes in the corners,
With hinges and ice-cold paper clips.

Shannon Reid (11)
Leigh Primary School, Tonbridge

The Two Sides Of Christmas

On the inside of Christmas dreams are becoming true,
On the outside it seems Jesus is only touching a few,
On the inside sparkling snow is being admired,
On the outside hungry children are cold and tired,
On the inside presents are being carefully picked,
On the outside children are lonely and sick,
On the inside it's almost time for bed,
On the outside the parents are searching for food to be fed,
On the inside food is being eaten while it's still hot,
On the outside they have no food so its not,
On the inside its time to take the decorations down,
On the outside it's still quiet in the sleepy town,
On the inside they've lit the glowing fire,
On the outside they just want to admire,
So when you are enjoying your Christmas treat,
Remember those with cold, sore feet.

Anna Chapman (11)
Leigh Primary School, Tonbridge

Fireworks, Fireworks

Fireworks, fireworks
Lighting up the sky
Bangers on the ground
And rockets flying high
Catherine wheels on sticks and fire burning bright
All are delights on Guy Fawkes Night.

Sarah-Jane Levings (11)
Leigh Primary School, Tonbridge

The Magic Box

(Based by 'Magic Box' by Kit Wright)

I will put in my box . . .

The gentle twitch of a rabbit touching a carrot
A jet-black engine zooming into space,
The taste of a croissant touching my taste buds.

I will put in my box . . .

The most famous pop star you could ever imagine,
A spirit rising from a four-poster bed,
The hardest sum in the world.

I will put in my box . . .

The biggest theme park in the world
The smelliest tramp around
The hottest country having a snowstorm.

I will put in my box . . .

A whale swimming on the beach
The fanciest clothes worn by an urchin
The ripest oranges having no juice in them.

I will put in my box . . .

The song of the rarest bird
The tallest tree in the universe
The shout of the loudest person

My box is icy cold.
It has boiling hinges
And dragon scales are shining on it like jewels.

Chloe Foster (10)
Licensed Victuallers' School, Ascot

The Magic Box

(Based by 'Magic Box' by Kit Wright)

I will put in my box . . .
Elegant elaborate eagles eminently soaring expeditiously,
Sapphires sitting spectacularly still, shining superbly,
Waxy weltering whales swimming wonderfully.

I will put in my box . . .
A huge egg of a dinosaur
Shimmering snow from the tip of Mount Everest
A shoot emerging from an acorn.

I will put in my box . . .
The first falling leaf from an ancient oak,
The last snowflake to fall at Christmas,
One diamond lamp granting three wishes.

I will put in my box . . .
Goldfish in the Mediterranean,
Fish in the sky and birds in the sea,
Evergreen trees with no leaves.

My box is fashioned from glass and silver
Diamond stars on all of the sides
And cactus thorns in the corners
Its hinges are the beaks of ancient birds

I shall ski in my box on the snowy Himalayas,
I shall jump through the clouds
And land in the sea with a splash!

James Chapman (10)
Licensed Victuallers' School, Ascot

The Magic Box

(Based by 'Magic Box' by Kit Wright)

I will put in my box . . .
The spectacular slash of a Samurai's sword
The invincible ice of immortality
The blaze of a burning bonfire

I will put in my box . . .
A magic twinkle of a sparkling bird
A magic wish of a newborn child
A final glimpse of a full moon
An imaginary friend

I will put in my box . . .
The first beat of a newborn heart
The beauty of life
The last gunshot from a world of war

I will put in my box . . .
A black heart with no emotion
A war with no men
A body with no organs

My box is made from gold
The finest silver with a fiery sheen
A shield of ice and a divine smell
More powerful than all the flowers in the World

I shall make a World of peace in my box
I shall create a god to control this World
I shall watch my new World and smile upon my new creation.

Tim Allison (10)
Licensed Victuallers' School, Ascot

The Magic Box

(Based by 'Magic Box' by Kit Wright)

I will put in my box . . .

A dying dragon dreading death
The blow from the wind on a chilly night
A small, slithering, scaly snake in the hot desert

I will put in my box . . .

A red-hot meteor heading for the Earth
A gold violin playing soft, soothing music

I will put in my box . . .

Seven ruby-red cushions all new and fluffy
The last drop of water from a well
The first glimpse of daylight in a new year

I will put in my box . . .

Superman playing football
David Beckham saving the world

My box was created with clear glass,
The hinges are made from steel
The secrets are deep down, and can't be told.

I will play in my box, and watch everything that comes past me
I will enjoy my box and I will never tell its secrets.

Edward Slegg (10)
Licensed Victuallers' School, Ascot

Magic Box

(Based by 'Magic Box' by Kit Wright)

I will put in my box . . .
The melting of marshmallows on
A shimmering winter's day,
The touch of a white, sparkling rabbit
Hopping round the garden
The shouting of my brother and me
So cross but sweet at the same time.

I will put in my box . . .
A warming smile on a freezing cold day
A tear of joy from my sister on Christmas Eve
A soft, warm bed keeping me warm throughout the night.

I will put in my box . . .
The gale of wind from east west China
Sapphire stars and a ruby moon swimming around the dark blue sky
The clear safe water we drink every day.

My box is made from ivory, rubies and diamond stars
A cat face keyhole
Paint from India
Numbers and letters carved into the lid
A gold rabbit with a ruby eye on top of my box!

Becky Stark (10)
Licensed Victuallers' School, Ascot

The Magic Box

(Based by 'Magic Box' by Kit Wright)

I will put in my box . . .
The excitement of a jet-black cat rushing after a Russian mouse
Three lucky sneezes flying across the Atlantic
A shimmering diamond

I will put in my box . . .
A paintbrush swirling around in the beautiful shimmering red paint
An ice cube freezing the mouth of a human

I will put in my box . . .
A balloon filled with magical orange dust
A silent aeroplane flying through the white clouds

I will put in my box . . .
A unicorn's horn glistening in the darkness
A dark brown cowboy boot
The sounds of snow trickling down the mountain when it rains.

My box is made of unicorn's teeth and all the colours of the rainbow.

Hattie Price (10)
Licensed Victuallers' School, Ascot

Guess Who?

The tail that flows from side to side,
The ears that twitch in great surprise,
The paws so delicate they make no sound,
The eyes that glow when new things are found,
The whiskers that prick in a gentle way,
The body that sleeps for half the day,
What is this creature? I'll let you decide.
The problem is it's already died.

Sadie Banyard (11)
Lytchett Matravers Primary School, Poole

A Sparkling Life Of Belief

Listen, listen, beyond the normal world,
What do you *now* hear?
A leprechaun galloping?
The dragons *raging*?
A creature the immortal fear?

Look, look, beyond the human eye,
What do you *now* see?
A lonely spirit drifting past?
Tiny sprites,
Eating a tiny tea?

Look at these words and listen,
Listen to what I'm saying to you.
If you believe in all magic,
You'll have the spark of life in whatever you do.

Lauren Murray (10)
Lytchett Matravers Primary School, Poole

If Only I Had Tidied My Room

Running, running
I think it's coming
Running through the street,
My heart is pounding,
Eardrums drumming,
I'm rushed off my feet,
It's purple and green,
It is not to be seen.
My mum is coming,
If only I had tidied my room!

Victoria Day (11)
Lytchett Matravers Primary School, Poole

Salad!

The smell and taste,
Won't go to waste,
I'm absolutely starving,
I can hear the knife carving,
I wonder what we've got for tea today,
If it's pizza, oh hip hip hooray!
I can't wait to see,
What mum's made for tea,
That's the beeper, a sign to come in,
If I don't go now, I'll get awfully thin.
But I came into a nasty surprise,
I couldn't believe my big blue eyes,
We had salad that night,
It caused a riot,
Mum told me we were going on a diet
And to this day I'm as thin as a stick
And the thought of a salad is making me sick!

Evie Rubenstein (10)
Lytchett Matravers Primary School, Poole

Beatroot

Boop, bop, bang, boom,
The drums beat *bang* below the big moon
A-shake, shake, shakalaka ching
They all spring up and start to sing.

A-crack, shack what a sound
The sun beats down upon the hot ground
A-song, kong, a-beep, bap, bong,
They all *bing-bang* a beatroot song.

A-chick, quick, a-boom, boom bastic,
The root of the beat is just fantastic!

Olivia Batchelor (11)
Lytchett Matravers Primary School, Poole

The Sight Of Parents Kissing

The sight of parents kissing
Is very well worth missing,
Mum you are getting older
And my body's getting colder
Oh, stop,
Please, stop.

The sight of parents kissing
Is very well worth missing
In the hall, on the stairs,
In the doorway, on the chairs
Forget about it,
Just forget about it.

The sight of parents kissing
Is very well worth missing
Listen to me, it really is!

Laura Burgess (11)
Lytchett Matravers Primary School, Poole

Nonsense

I woke up this morning and the cat was on my head!
I woke up this morning and the toys walked off my bed,
I woke up this morning and my toast started talking,
I woke up this morning and my fork started walking.

I walked to school this morning still in my PJs,
I walked to school this morning thinking it wasn't May,
I walked to school this morning and I walked into a post,
I walked to school this morning and a monster started to boast.

I walked straight home this morning and really banged my head,
I walked through the door this morning; I think I'll go back to bed!

Charlotte Tummon (11)
Lytchett Matravers Primary School, Poole

Guess Who!

She creeps,
She crawls,
She scratches at the walls.

Her whiskers flounce,
Her eyelids flicker,
Her favourite food - mmm - kipper!

She'll pounce
She'll bound,
She'll run 'til found.

I'll file my nails
I'll wash my paws
I'll always break the feline laws!

Have you guessed who I am?
My name is Purr-sephone,
There's another clue . . .
I'll leave the rest up to you!

Answer: cat!

Chloë Matthews (11) & Holly Dent (10)
Lytchett Matravers Primary School, Poole

Ekans

I swirl,
I wriggle,
I slither,
I may tickle,
You would find me in a jungle,
All curled up in a bundle,
If I slithered backwards,
I might be called Ekans
What am I?

Sam Smithard (10)
Lytchett Matravers Primary School, Poole

The Flying Goats

Here come the flying goats,
I don't know how they float,
Here comes the flying pig,
And he is wearing a rather strange wig.
Here comes the flying cat,
Whatever happened to the flying mat?
Here come the flying dogs,
And why are they wearing clogs?
Here comes the flying ape,
He is wearing a black and red cape.
Here come the flying sheep,
Their voices are very deep.

Those are my flying animals,
And no they are not cannibals.

Thomas Holmes (11)
Lytchett Matravers Primary School, Poole

Dolphins

Dolphins diving through the sea
I gaze in wonder from the quay
Up and down
Round and round
Dolphins splashing
Sea crashing
Tails thumping
Gracefully jumping
Horn blows
Oh no!
Ship clatters
Dolphin scatters
The ship gave them a fright
But they'll be back tomorrow night.

Coco Moore (11)
Lytchett Matravers Primary School, Poole

A Visit To The Church

Light blue skies as you walk down the lanes,
Down to the church with its dark windowpanes.

The tower a stubby finger, old,
Pointing the way to Heaven, 'Behold!'
The sole survivor of forgotten plague,
Humble and cosy, tucked away,
Worshippers gone as the years have sped,
Losing the living, gaining the dead.

Yellow peach sun shines down on Earth,
Spring is a time of life's rebirth
Gravestones being swallowed into the soil,
All that's left from a life of toil.

Soldiers on a frozen march,
Their uniforms grey, stiff as starch,
The new gravestones bright and shiny,
With sad little toys on the graves of the tiny!

Pippa Woods (11)
Lytchett Matravers Primary School, Poole

Universe

Bright sunlit moon,
Green blue Earth
Cold freezing Pluto,
Burning hot Mars
Enormous growing Neptune
Massive blistering Venus,
Tiny little Mercury,
Ringed giant Saturn,
Ugly grey Uranus,
Huge bold Jupiter.

Beware the sun is about to blow.

Jayden Stockley (11)
Lytchett Matravers Primary School, Poole

Why Football Rules

Football is a fantastic sport,
The pitch is bigger than a tennis court,
There are lots of different young stars,
Better than all the golf stars pars.

Johnny Wilkinson's worse than David Beckham,
Some players come from Peckham,
A left or right back
Can run fast down an athletics track.

There are lots of different positions,
In a transfer window, teams have some additions,
Football isn't a small sport, it's big,
It's better than working on an oilrig.

So now can you see why football
Rules!

Liam Collins (10)
Lytchett Matravers Primary School, Poole

Morning Break

It's morning break,
I've got nothing to do.
'How can you have nothing to do?' you ask me,
'Look at all the other children playing happily.'

I don't like them, they don't like me,
I try to play but they say, 'Go away,
We don't like you, you don't like us,'
And they go on like that, making such a fuss.

So I go and sit in a corner,
It's quite nice to be alone,
It's a beautiful day,
So why don't I play?
I don't know.

James Shannon (11)
Lytchett Matravers Primary School, Poole

The Seasons

Autumn is red,
Leaves form a bed
On the ground
Whilst the time flies around.

Winter is cold and harsh,
The snow is falling fast,
The fires are on,
The hot summer's sun has gone.

Spring is here,
Baby lambs, foals and deer,
New life has arrived
Along with food which has thrived.

Summer is hot
Ice cream in a pot,
Sunbathing too,
I had a nice time. Did you?

Beth Duncan (11)
Lytchett Matravers Primary School, Poole

Daisy Chain

Daisies are sweet, pretty and small,
They don't create trouble at all,
But when it comes to daisy chains,
Well that's another story,
They scream and shout and cry when you come to make your chain.
And when you play the
'He loves me, he loves me not' game
They beg you to *stop! Stop! Stop!*
So just look at the sweet little daisy
And think to yourself
Is it really worth destroying a flower?
For your daisy chain?
Or for your prince charming?

Daisy Miles (11)
Lytchett Matravers Primary School, Poole

Seasons

Spring . . .
Where are the bunnies bouncing everywhere?
Where are the flowers breathing in our air?
Where are the lambs jumping in their pens?
Where are the chicks, are they with the hens?

Summer . . .
Here are the apples, all ripe and green,
Here are the deckchairs, cool, blue and clean,
Here is the corn, tied up in sheaves,
Here is the oak, laden down with leaves.

Autumn . . .
Gone are the leaves, falling to the ground,
Gone are the acorns that the squirrel found,
Gone is the hedgehog, he's off for a nap,
Gone is the bikini, replaced by coat and cap.

Winter . . .
There is a blanket, not warm but of snow,
There is a robin, cold from where the north wind blows,
There is the holly tied up in a wreath,
There is the Christmas tree with presents underneath.

Abigail Horlock (11)
Lytchett Matravers Primary School, Poole

Spiralling Sports

Dribble, turn,
Swerve, pass,
The referee looks so stern
Three, two, one, *shoot!*
You score a goal!

Cartwheel, roll,
Spin, stop,
You see the floor as burning coal,
Three, two, one, *sprint!*
You've won the gold!

Step, hop,
Point, spring,
Concentrate, do not stop
Three, two, one, *spin!*
You've passed!

Skid, skate,
Balance, speed,
The ice is fine, you're not too late,
Three, two, one, *twirl!*
The judges mark you 10, 10, 10!

Yasmin Farasat (11)
Lytchett Matravers Primary School, Poole

Miss Whizz Bang Whirly Pop

Miss Whizz Bang Whirly Pop,
Y'know, that nutter with the bike?
Yep, I guess you've guessed it too,
I'm her poor grandson Mike.

It's always been so embarrassing,
When she whizzes down the lane,
No wonder passers-by think my granny's insane!

The purple hair,
The wacky boots,
The body piercings,
But worst of all,
The motorbike that toots!

It's all a bit too much,
For a granny,
Don't you think?
A lot of people do,
But I don't think so,
I think she's cool,
Go granny, you rule!

Olivia Sawyer (10)
Lytchett Matravers Primary School, Poole

The Detachable Body

As I was walking down the street
I realised I had no feet,
I spun around in time to see
My fingers scuttling up a tree.
I couldn't believe what I'd just seen,
It couldn't be real, it must be a dream!
It was true, I realised with a sickening thud
When I saw that my arms were now rolling in mud.
I yelled and I yelled, surely someone would hear,
When out of the pub came a drunk with a beer,
He thought it was funny, he laughed himself red,
Then he got out a meat axe and chopped off my head.
I began to despair, what on earth should I do?
When I saw a young man with some super-strong glue.
He came over to me, gave a short little chuckle,
And helped me out of my embarrassing muddle,
He decided to do his good deed for the day,
He stuck me together, then just walked away.
Now readers the moral of this story is you
Should always make sure you've a spare pot of glue.

David Hayward (11)
Lytchett Matravers Primary School, Poole

My Friends

My friend Hannah
Walks like a spanner

My friend Jenny
Has a penny

My friend Holly May
Loves the smell of hay

My friend Jack
Needs a good smack

My friend Nick
Looks like a stick

My friend Millie
Has a sister called Tille

My mate Izzy
Is always dizzy.

These are all my friends and they are weird but I don't care!

Sammy Griffiths (10)
Lytchett Matravers Primary School, Poole

Tigers, Tigers

Tigers, tigers are so powerful
And they are so wonderful,
Tigers like to play
In the hay.

Tigers, tigers are so scary,
And they get so hairy,
Tigers look up at the sky
While eating pie.

Ben Cousins (10)
Micklands Primary School, Caversham

A Puppy's Life

There was a young puppy called Squawk
Who enjoyed going out for a walk,
But he preferred sitting at home,
Whilst chewing his bone,
As he and his brothers would talk.

There was a teenage puppy called Squawk
Who always licked his chalk,
But he was too old to draw,
So he sat on the floor,
While he gobbled up his pork.

There was an old puppy called Squawk,
Who wanted to live in New York,
But he had no money,
For he lived on honey,
And he was best friends with a hawk.

There was a dead puppy called Squawk,
Who could no longer talk,
But he couldn't keep still,
Because he felt ill,
So he wandered out for a walk.

Gemma Thomas (10)
Micklands Primary School, Caversham

My Car

My engine is a dog growling at a cat,
My rims are the sparkling sun,
My tinted windows are like a black bat,
My exhausts, I have two not one.
My wide body kit makes it look fat,
Driving in my car it's lots of fun.

Klein Mason (11)
Micklands Primary School, Caversham

Smile

I nearly always smile,
I smile when I play,
I smile when I'm happy,
I smile every day.

I smile when I'm yappy,
I smile when I care,
I smile when I laugh,
I smile at the fair.

I smile when I'm at the park,
I smile when I'm kind,
I smile when I dance,
And when I lose my mind.

I smile when I have a chance,
I smile when I play with toys,
I smile when I sleep,
I smile when there's noise.

I smile when the tides are deep,
I smile when I'm having fun,
I smile when I have a friend,
I smile when I'm in the sun.

I smile when I'm at a dead end,
I smile when I'm at school,
I smile at good and bad times,
I don't know why at all!

Emily Cousins (10)
Micklands Primary School, Caversham

Seasons

Spring is a wonderful thing,
A few April showers,
To water the flowers,
Oh, it just wants to make me sing!

Summer is the time
To go away and camp
There is a big problem if the ground is damp
Oh, it's just divine to make myself rhyme.

Autumn is when the leaves fall
Down to the ground
And all around
The trees stand bare and tall.

Winter is cold
When it snows
The midnight moon it glows and glows
The autumn days are old.

Sam Cuss (11)
Micklands Primary School, Caversham

The Seaside

Stormy night out in the sea,
Thundering waves roaring at me,
Darkening more over me,
Sand as still as can be,
I am as scared as can be,
There's nobody here to help me.

Kymm Sessions (11)
Micklands Primary School, Caversham

The Silver Dragon

The silver dragon flies in the ancient sky
With wings of shimmering silver.

His huge bulky body dwarfs you and me
Especially when he lands on the ground.

His teeth are as sharp as steak knives
Which help him devour flesh and blood!

His tail twists and turns behind him
When he is soaring through the air.

The fire that he breathes glistens with silver
Which helps him to burn down thick lush forests.

His head is similar to that of a crocodiles,
Which makes him look terrifying.

James Peedell (11)
Micklands Primary School, Caversham

Sunny Seasons

S himmering sun shining through the clouds,
U nder umbrellas to keep the sun off me,
M arvellous meals from holidays afar,
M elting marshmallows upon the barbecue,
E vil rain flies away to another country,
R unning rapidly to the school field.

S hining sun sleeping upon the clouds,
P retty poppies growing as tall as you,
R oses ringing around the sun,
I walk to the school gate waiting for the teachers,
N aughty rain comes along,
G orgeous goat having a baby in the barn.

Amy Wells (10)
Micklands Primary School, Caversham

The Theme Park

There are some rides that go upside down,
There are some rides that go round and round,
There are some rides that go up and down,
There are some rides that go near to the ground.

There's lots of drinks and food,
There's ice cream for when you're in the mood,
There are lots of things to buy,
Like souvenirs and chocolate bars.

There are some rides that immediately drop,
There are some rides that immediately stop,
There are some rides that make you sick,
After eating ice cream on a stick.

There is also stuff to do,
There's chuck a basket ball through a hoop,
There are some prizes just like that,
A mighty duck and a pat on the back.

There are some rides that make you excited,
There are some things that make you delighted,
There are some rides that will give you a scare,
But you can go on them if you dare.

Craig Spicer (10)
Micklands Primary School, Caversham

Families

F amiliar faces at special celebrations,
A ll the children having fun on holiday vacations,
M ost of them live miles away,
I don't see them often, but that's OK,
L urking round the town with my brother,
I f I'm good, he won't call Mother,
E ven though he never comes home,
S ometimes he replies to the phone!

Melissa Campbell (11)
Micklands Primary School, Caversham

A Flying Pig

You'll never guess what I saw today,
Lots of people said, 'No way!'
A flying pig in the sky
Scoffing down a custard pie.

The big fat pig flew over my head
He stole my dad's new moped,
I tried to catch him but he was too fast
He had the radio on full blast!

The big pink thing stopped at a red light,
I tried to get him off; he packs a nasty bite,
A policeman came he looked furious,
The big pink pig, he looked very curious.

The silly pig, he got arrested
He was riding without being tested
If someone asks you didn't you hear it from me!
So excuse me now it's time for PE.

Sally Russell (11)
Micklands Primary School, Caversham

The Garbage Bin

My sister's known as 'the garbage bin',
She'll eat just about anything,
From a tiny carrot to an apple pie,
She'll eat it all in the blink of an eye.

I bet she could eat a whole chocolate cake,
As well as a great big juicy steak,
I wonder if she'd like some vanilla ice cream?
What about a big toffee dream!

Christie Gillatt (9)
Micklands Primary School, Caversham

About The Arsenal Squad

Number one is Lehmann, when he gets fouled he shouts, 'Hey man!'
Number two, don't know who.
Number three is Cole, he loves to score a goal,
Number four is Vieira, he likes to tackle Alan Shearer,
Number five took the dive,
Number six took free kicks,
Number seven is Pires, he crosses it in for Reyes,
Number eight is Fredrik, he needs to get a hat-trick,
Number nine is Reyes, he's great pals with Pires,
Number ten is Dennis, he prefers tennis,
Number eleven is Van Persie, he wants to hear another Versie,
Number twelve is Lauren, he gets in there to score 'em.
Number thirteen has a cinema screen,
Number fourteen is the best - Henry, he got a cross from me.
Number fifteen is Fabregas, I think he likes t o play the bass.

Jake Bicknell (11)
Micklands Primary School, Caversham

The School Nurse Called Miss Janet

Bottles, ointments, sticky plasters
For the terrible disasters
She uses these on bleeding knees.

Healing us with care like a cuddly bear.

Miss J is kind
She has the greatest mind
She has a big heart
Uses it on Bart.

She's healing us with care like a cuddly bear.

Lavana Raza (9)
Micklands Primary School, Caversham

My Family

My mum and dad are there for me
They let me invite my friends for tea
They're getting me this; they're getting me that
Sometimes it's nice to have a chat
It's not just the things that were bought
It's love and caring
They bought the clothes that I'm wearing
As well as the shoes on my feet
As well as the food that I eat
Those are the things that make me glad
I have a loving mum and dad

Brothers are great
But sometimes we hate
It's nice to have fun
But sometimes I run
Away from my little brother
Here I am writing this poem, so much
I want to show him

Grandparents are good
Sometimes they're misunderstood
Of the way I live my childhood.

Jamie Gray (10)
Micklands Primary School, Caversham

The Garden

'Twas the back of the garden,
Where the sound of young children drifted away,
The sound of doors creaking in the background,
Dogs howling with the wind,
Dried out flowers which have been forgotten,
Worn out grass,
Down at the back of the garden.

'Twas the centre of the garden,
Where flowers swayed in the breeze,
The sound of high-pitched laughter in the distance,
The dog traipsed across the flowers,
Dried up leaves on the ground,
Worn out trees,
Down at the centre of the garden.

'Twas the start of the garden,
Where the children ran wild,
The sound of a door slamming shut.
Dogs running free,
Dried out clothes hanging on the line,
Worn out flowers,
At the start of the garden.

Stephanie-Rose Ball (11)
Micklands Primary School, Caversham

Strange Animals

There once was a monkey named Tok,
Who didn't like to smash any rocks,
He turned into a mouse.
And went into a house,
And now he's climbing the clock.

There was a young weasel called Otter,
Who didn't like to read Harry Potter,
The others read books,
And so they took
To calling young weasel 'The Rotter'.

There once was a tiger named Mint,
Who approved of his car in a red tint,
It attracted a bull,
Who rammed it into a wall
And now the car's made of flint.

There once was a lion called Mane,
Who was always in a lot of pain,
He got into fights
That was always very tight,
But now he's become very tame.

Alex Clark (11)
Micklands Primary School, Caversham

Things I Like

Ashley Cole,
Scored a goal,

The Mighty Rock
Put Kane in a head lock,

Frodo and Sam in 'Lord of the Rings',
We're saved by birds with big wings,

Kevin in 'Home Alone'
Makes bandits moan,

If you drive fast cars,
Then you will go behind bars.

In 'Cheaper By The Dozen'
They have lots of cousins.

Ross Newport-Dempster (9)
Napier CP School, Gillingham

A Trip To The Sea

I love going to the sea,
It fills me with glee.
I watch the waves leap
As I find shiny shells that I can keep.
I hear the sea breath in and out
As I watch the children play about.
The cliffs tower around me
It's like they're hungry.
The fish glide,
As I say my goodbyes,
I am now leaving the sea.

Shauna Mansbridge (11)
Northolmes Junior School, Horsham

Storm At Sea

I perched myself on a rock,
On the shore and just gazed at the deep blue sea,
It was only I on the beach,
Alone in the twilight,
The calm ocean overlapped the coarse grains of sand,
A slight drizzle descended from the moonlit sky,
Thunder growled in the distance like a rottweiler dog,
Lightning clapped like the dog's snapping jaws.

This only meant one thing,
A storm,
By now the storm was monstrous,
The thunder *roared* over the face of the ocean,
I dived for cover but the wave got me first,

And the last thing I saw was a lighthouse light . . .

Daniel Randon (11)
Northolmes Junior School, Horsham

Vicious Wind

'Why are you so cruel? Blistering my eyes,
You angry brute vicious, mean and sly.'

'Why are you so destructive? Tearing down trees,
You're howling with happiness as everybody flees.'

'I came because nature calls me every day
You all have friends and now it's my turn to play.'

Aaron Czajkowska (11)
Northolmes Junior School, Horsham

Emotions

'Whisper, whisper,'
Said the sea,
I sometimes feel
It's calling to me.

But sometimes it cries
And I feel weak,
I cannot give it
Comfort it may seek.

Sometimes it's angry
And sends vicious waves,
I cannot give it
The counsel it craves.

But sometimes it's happy,
A calm breeze will blow
And at times like this
You can never feel low.

Nicole Barnes (11)
Northolmes Junior School, Horsham

I Want To See The Sea

'Mum, I want to see the sea, the roaring wavy sea.'
'No, no it's too cold to see the sea, the roaring wavy sea.'
'Mum, I want to see the sea, the cold and windy sea.'
'No, no it's too dark to see the cold and windy sea.'
'Mum, I want to see the sea, the rough and bumpy sea.'
'No, no it's raining you can't see the sea, the rough and bumpy sea.'
'Mum, I want to see the sea, the shiny, dutiful sea.'
'Yes, you can see the sea, the shiny, dutiful sea.'

Emma Rickman (11)
Northolmes Junior School, Horsham

The Hurricane

Twisting, turning in the air,
Messing up people's hair,
Pulling, tugging, it destroys,
Sucking up the children's toys,
Baying, growling, vicious hound,
Silence filled with howling sounds,
Swerving, flexing it chases me,
I crouch and hid, I cannot flee.

Lauren Jones (11)
Northolmes Junior School, Horsham

Tsunami

The people dying in the sea of water,
Parents losing a son or daughter,
Drowning, sinking, losing air,
Flooding the country without a care.
Delicate lives hanging by a thread,
Not all will survive, some will be dead.
Waves crashing one by one,
No way to escape, nowhere to run.

Chloe Fletcher (11)
Northolmes Junior School, Horsham

Wasp

W arrier brave and strong
A ngry child
S uper speed
P erfect soldier.

Matthew Trotman (11)
Northolmes Junior School, Horsham

Under The Sea

'What are you, Sea?
Are you rain that hasn't dried?'
'No, I am the sea.'

'Why are you jagged, Sea
Like the spikes on barbed wire?'
'It's the wind that blows me.'

'How did you get here, Sea
By bus or by aeroplane?'
'No, I came by rain.'

'When did you get here, Sea,
Yesterday or a year ago?'
'No, I came millions of years ago.'

Jamie-Leigh Price (11)
Northolmes Junior School, Horsham

Peace

Peace is when you can relax,
Not having to worry about things like tax.
Some people's peace is a beautiful sight,
But to others it is the evening light.

A peaceful place can be anywhere,
Somewhere with shade, clear seas or a comfy chair.
Somewhere with palm trees or soft, clean sand,
Somewhere that you could call your own homeland.

The best time for peace is at the crack of dawn,
But remember peace is fragile and is easily torn.

Emma Hollingworth (11)
Northolmes Junior School, Horsham

The Sea

The sea is like a glistening jewel,
It keeps on going, it's not small.

The sea changes rapidly,
Go there, wait and see.

The sea breathes in and out,
When the soggy seagulls screech and shout.

The sea is like a great creature,
It was the first living; teaching others like a teacher.

The sea is never lonely at night,
Because it scrunches up tight!

Lauren Hale (10)
Northolmes Junior School, Horsham

A Day Out To The Seaside

S eagulls screeching like dolphins having fun.
E very child playing,
A nd enjoying the sun.
S andcastles building on the seashore.
I n every corner are people visiting from different countries
    having a sea tour.
D ays have passed and have been forgotten,
    I'm going to treasure this day.
E veryone's forgotten, but I still remember the 27th of May.

Rebecca Loughnane (11)
Northolmes Junior School, Horsham

Underneath The Surface

Underneath the surface
There's a secret mystic world,
Creatures swimming round
Whirl, whirl, whirl.

Underneath the surface
There's a mermaid swimming gently,
Seaweed swishing through her tail
Swish, swish, swish.

Underneath the surface
There's an oyster with its pearl,
Bubbles popping in and out
Pop, pop, pop.

Underneath the surface
There's a sparkling rainbow fish,
Glimmering in the sunshine
Twinkle, twinkle, twinkle.

Underneath the surface
There's a shark with giant teeth,
Grabbing other fish
Snap, snap, snap.

Alice Jarvis (10)
Northolmes Junior School, Horsham

Sea Poems

What I see is the deep blue,
And that's what I want to see,
The deep blue sea.

The sea has got a beauty like a sunset.
The sea has got force like an angry lion.
The sea started life for all of us.

Crash-whoosh,
Crash-whoosh,
Crash-whoosh,
I love you sea!

Nothing can compare to you, sea
Except the taste of ice cream.

The sea is cooling
The sea sparkles all night long, *wow!*
I've got to go, sea.

Devon Watson (11)
Northolmes Junior School, Horsham

The Seaweed

S ea is like something running towards you
   and pushing you over on your back,
E veryone should love the sea, there are lots of things
   you can do and play on at the seaside,
A nd there are lots of different animals in the sea,
   different colours, different shapes,
W ater is being splashed around by lots of children
   playing and laughing,
E ach child is playing on the beach or in sea or eating their lunch,
E very wave crashing into the shore and rocks,
D ozens of boats are on the sea.

Sophie Lebba (12)
Northolmes Junior School, Horsham

Why Are You So . . . ?

'Why are you so deep, Sea?
What secrets have you got to keep, Sea?
Why don't you have any feet, Sea?'

'Because I am not one of you.'

'Why are you so wet, Sea?
What fish have you met, Sea?'

'I have met all fish inside of me.'

'Why are you blue, Sea?'

'It's not me, it's the sky.'

One more question,
What makes your waves leap?'

*'It's not me, it's the plates
Inside of me.'*

Christopher Cakebread (10)
Northolmes Junior School, Horsham

Sea Poem

'Why are you salty, Sea?'
'It's the chlorine under me.'
'Why are you so deep, Sea?'
'It's for the fishes to have an adventure.'

'Why are you so rough, Sea?'
'It's not me, it's the plates crashing together under me.'
'Why is your colour blue, Sea?'
'It's not me, it's the reflection from the sun.'

'Why do you have waves, Sea?'
'It's the wind running over me.'
'Why are you not clear, Sea?'
'You can't keep a secret from me!'

Oliver Salmon (11)
Northolmes Junior School, Horsham

An Avalanche

An avalanche is a hungry lion,
Stalking quietly,
Prey unaware,
A mighty roar, the only warning,
Before pouncing,
Instantaneous death.

Down, down, down it comes,
Its victims at its mercy.

It covers itself in a white coat,
Hiding the terror of this mighty beast,
As it comes down the hill to consume its feast,
Some boulders roll, others fly,
But whatever the outcome, people will die.

Down, down, down it comes,
Its victims at its mercy.

Ross Walden (11)
Northolmes Junior School, Horsham

The Beach

B eautiful blue waves are hurled at the shore,
E ach wave strolls and clashes against the rocks
   like cymbals being crashed,
A nd the jagged waves roar,
C hildren splashing and playing in the crystal clear blue sea,
H aving fun in the sun is not against the law!

Chelsea Johnson (11)
Northolmes Junior School, Horsham

The Hairdressers!

'Eddie, time to go to the hairdressers!'
'No! Hair doesn't want to dress now.'
'No Eddie, they cut your hair, come on let's go and catch the bus.'
'No? Come on.'
'Can I take Bob The Builder?'
'Yes, you can take your teddy.'
'No! Not teddy, Bob The Builder!'
'OK, come on, we'll be late.'
'OK! We'll be late.'
'How long is it?'
'What do you mean Eddie?'
'How long does it take to get there?'
'About 5 minutes.'
'Can I get a lolly? I need one!'
'Another day Eddie.'
'Mummy, I need the potty!'
'We're nearly there!'
'But I can't wait!'
'Two more minutes.'
'Whoopsy!'

Jessica Ball (10)
Northolmes Junior School, Horsham

Slugs

S lugs slither everywhere
L eaving slime on garden chairs,
U nder sheds and over stones,
G obbling flowers as they go,
S lugs slither everywhere.

Rebecca Rickman (11)
Northolmes Junior School, Horsham

Why Are You?

'Why are you blue Sea?
Why are you so popular in a hot summer?'
'I really want to know why they will not let me be.'

'Why are you so jumpy, Sea?
Why do you shine the light?'
'It's because the sun and the moon grow over me.'

'I compared you to a swimming pool, why are you the best, Sea?'
'Kids love you, why is that?'
'Kids love me for who I am, not for what I do.'

'How many sea animals do you know, Sea?
Are you mean or are you nice?'
'They're OK, some act like my big sisters.'

'How do you make friends, Sea?
Wow, you really are wonderful, don't you think?'
'Not really, I have been like this all my life.'

'What do you have for tea, Sea?
Is it different to my world?'
'I have seaweed.'

Louise Barnard (11)
Northolmes Junior School, Horsham

Leopard

L ively
E vil
O ffensive
P ouncing
A ngry
R oaring
D eadly cats.

Katie Heath (10)
Northolmes Junior School, Horsham

Chevrolet

C hevrolet only the best
H eavy powered metal, you'll be impressed
E verybody wants to drive
V 8 engine noisy and alive
R oaring down the highway
O ver hills and far away
L eaving smiles in the air
E very person stops and stares,
T ruly it's the finest car of all.

Lucy Martlew (11)
Northolmes Junior School, Horsham

Ice

Ice freezes the land on a cold winter's night,
Early next morning it doesn't leave without a fight.

Ice covers countries during cold seasons,
Children play with it for no such reason.

Ice gleams on tall mountains all year long,
When winter has finished it is all gone.

Jake Gallard (11)
Northolmes Junior School, Horsham

Seas And Oceans

S even oceans in the world,
E asy to spot on a map of the world,
A tlantic is an ocean,
S o many seas and oceans.

Josh Tustin (11)
Northolmes Junior School, Horsham

The Dragon

In the tower there sat a dragon,
It was huge, 100 times bigger than a wagon,
Roaring fiercely, the dragon flew down,
Into the petrified town,
It set alight the palace roof,
Which was gone in one poof.
Then a knight came through, his armour black,
And a javelin he carried on his back.
He drew it very quickly,
The dragon gulped and looked at it sickly,
The knight threw it at the beast,
Which made for the town an excellent feast,
So that was that, the knight fled east,
Where he slayed another beast.

Dan Maguire (10)
Northolmes Junior School, Horsham

The Day I Tricked My Teacher

My teacher went to her drawer,
To get some of her paper,
Then she went down to the office,
So I thought, I'll trick her later.

I crept to her box,
Quickly took the paper,
Put a toad in,
That will make her shout.

She opened the drawer,
And what a screech,
To my surprise . . .
She clapped her hands, smiled in delight and declared,
'Just what I've always wanted!'

Matthew Morrison (11)
Northolmes Junior School, Horsham

Nature

Nature is big and nature is small.
Nature is kind and nature is cruel.
Nature can be such a vicious bully
Especially when it's pushing and pulling.
Knocking trees over everywhere
Destroying lives without a care.
When nature decides to kill everyone
There is nowhere you can hide - nowhere you can run.

Laura Hollobon (10)
Northolmes Junior School, Horsham

Blitzed

B ombs flying everywhere,
L ondon citizens running scared
I nto the shelters quick now go!
T errible bombers flying down low
Z igzagging doodlebugs flying madly through the air
E veryone afraid of the World War II scare
D ambusters ready to fly 3, 2, 1 chocks away!

Aaron Moss (11)
Northolmes Junior School, Horsham

Nature

N othing is more powerful,
A ll is at its feet,
T he elements, fire, water, wind and earth
U nder the earth, above the earth, makes the world look sweet,
R eady, you have got to be,
E arthquakes shattering things that belong to me.

Ciara Spence (11)
Northolmes Junior School, Horsham

UFOs 'N' Space

UFOs fly overhead,
While Pluto has already fled.
Deep in outer space, far away,
A rocket had set off that day.
Now we find our station has gone,
And now we start to worry.
Was it the black hole that got it,
Or was it the comet that got it?
We wonder if we should explore.

Saturn sees the rocket,
He starts to battle.
Now Jupiter and Neptune,
With Uranus . . . they fail.
Here comes Mars,
Bringer of war.
He starts to battle,
He wins!

Nicholas Roberts (9)
St Catherine's RC Primary School, Bridport

Flowers

Flowers standing straight and tall,
Some are big, some are small,
Their petals are pretty in every way,
Even through the winter days,
When they grow old and frail,
And even when their colours pale,
They drop a seed to germinate,
Following sun and rain,
The plants will flower once again.

Eleanor Reynolds-Grey (9)
St Catherine's RC Primary School, Bridport

Football

Some things are good,
Some things are bad,
When it's good,
They all go mad
Guess what it is?
It's football!
But be careful,
It could be quite cruel.

Football is good,
Football is bad.
Though football's cool,
It can be cruel,
When it's kicking,
Missing, annoying
Or toying with another
Player who's now worrying
For his mother.

We've got to win,
We've got to score,
We can't afford
It to be a draw.
We need that cup
To hold up high,
To show our fans
We really did try.

Cameron Taylor (9)
St Catherine's RC Primary School, Bridport

Doctor Who

The Doctor travels through time and space
All dead are his alien race
Travelling in the Tardis killing all the Daleks
Cybermen
Are the biggest threat
But The Doctor has only met
A few yet.

In 2012 there are lots of space weapons
Only one worked out of all the seven
He took it to try and kill the Dalek
Because he thought
His friend Rose was dead
But the Dalek gave up
And self-destructed.

Troy Smith (8)
St Catherine's RC Primary School, Bridport

Tottenham Are OK!

Keane so clever,
Defoe is divine,
White is their colour
But is the keeper blind?
Mido is magical,
The manager so mighty.
Kanoute likes to kick out.
Although they're Spurs,
I guess they're OK.
But if you ask me,
It's Man U all the way!

Beth Donovan (9)
St Catherine's RC Primary School, Bridport

Arsenal Win The Champions League Against Chelsea

Arsenal have a penalty shootout and Lehmann is ready,
But Chelsea's goalkeeper was very steady.
Goals from Patrick as the crowd did roar,
Whereas Chelsea are looking very poor.
Now it's Chelsea's turn, which way will they shoot?
Whichever way they will, it will take a big boot.
Will Chelsea score and make it a draw
Or will they miss and Arsenal score more?
Nope, it's gone in the left-hand side,
The game's getting tense, as the score is all tied.
A few minutes later, the score's 4-all,
Arsenal's turn now will they whack the ball?
This is Chelsea's final chance,
Will they score or will Arsenal advance?
No, it's gone wide, I cannot believe it;
Arsenal's celebrating, tearing off their kit.
They're holding the cup up so proudly,
They hold it up high as the crowd cheer loudly.
Chelsea is upset, John starts crying,
But Arsenal I'm proud to say is absolutely flying.

Luke Antinoro (10)
St Catherine's RC Primary School, Bridport

A Spring Morning

Crisp under my feet,
The frosty buds crunched.
There on the seat I could see it all,
The cold and misty air was still,
The garden ghostly quiet,
Not a sound was broken,
Until . . .
Sunbeams penetrated the house beyond.

Alexandra Blanchard (9)
St Catherine's RC Primary School, Bridport

The War That Ended All Wars!

Alien invasion coming our way,
Somewhere in space,
Getting closer every day.
A satellite discovered a single trace,
Now threatening the existence of the human race.
Everywhere around,
Silence was drowned,
For screaming and shouting
Had struck the Earth's ground.
For the aliens were here,
And they'd come from the planet Sneer.

The men of Earth all came together,
As the battle was a perilous endeavour.
All the Earth's armies were sent in first,
But because of the dreadful aliens' thirst all of them perished,
As the aliens got the planet they cherished.

Rory Smith (10)
St Catherine's RC Primary School, Bridport

Southampton Football Club

I used to like Beattie, I thought he was great
Until he left for Everton, it's now too late
For Southampton to reclaim him it's just too hard,
He never sent us a letter, or even a card.
Matthew Le Tissier known as Le God,
Yes! Peter Crouch got picked in the England squad.
There was a lot of cheering when Harry Redknapp came,
Except for Pompey, they just called him names.
Jamie Redknapp also came and was called one name,
It was 'traitor', but instead he'll be scoring goals later.

Robert Evans (10)
St Catherine's RC Primary School, Bridport

Fireworks

Fireworks are banging,
Fizzing and whizzing,
Catherine wheels are turning,
Fireworks are whirling,
You will hear tremendous noises,
So remember, remember the 5th of November
When fireworks go mad!

All over the land you will hear screams, shouts and bangs
Those are music to a firework's ear,
So remember to clap your hands.

The fireworks get angry,
You will see how it is to scream,
But you know fireworks are harmless -
If you're one of them!
Hold your breath if you smell
Smoke, sizzles and pops,
Because that is the way fireworks *scream!*

Joseph Grew-McEvoy (9)
St Catherine's RC Primary School, Bridport

Sport

Many different people
Many different teams
Many different players
Living out their dreams
Seeing many talents
Not meeting many queens
Many different countries
Taking part in these events
Many different players
Making history out of their dreams
These are wonderful teams.

Michael Brown (9)
St Catherine's RC Primary School, Bridport

School

Another day at school,
More work,
Oh no!
Books, pencils, pens and rubbers,
Teachers looking in the cupboard,
Having maths,
Don't understand,
Finally the bell has rang.

Having a race,
With my friends,
How fun can it get?
I hope break never ends!

Leticia Ebben (10)
St Catherine's RC Primary School, Bridport

Aliens!

Far away, deep in space,
There lives a cruel alien race.
These aliens are clever and very small
But their rules are not fair at all.
Very quick, without a trace,
The flesh would be missing from your face.
In twenty seconds and nothing more,
There'll just be bones on the floor.
Have you heard of these creatures?
You will do soon
They're coming to a planet near you!

Oliver Hibbs (10)
St Catherine's RC Primary School, Bridport

The FA Cup Final

Finally it's kick-off, from pass to pass,
Oh look at that cross, it flew over the grass,
Just look at that header,
It flew through the weather,
What a save from the keeper,
I think it made him much weaker,
Here comes the rebound, what a goal!

It's kick-off for Man U,
With the Arsenal crowd shouting, *'Boo!'*
Man U passed down the line,
For Arsenal it's a very bad sign,
What if they score?
Will it end in a draw?
The final whistle has been blown,
It's now time to go home.
The Gunners have done it,
They've gone and won it.

Charlie Teideman (9)
St Catherine's RC Primary School, Bridport

Flowers

Flowers, flowers, they're so great
Some are wavy
Some are straight
Flowers, flowers, they're so bright
Red and yellow
Blue or even white
Pretty and colourful
Full of scent
Flowers, flowers, they're so fragrant.

Sophie Hall (9)
St Catherine's RC Primary School, Bridport

The Dog Called Spike

My dog is lazy,
My dog lies around,
Every time I look around,
The dog is on the ground.
He eats my sweets,
Bites holes in Mum's sheets,
Every time we go downstairs
The kitchen is a mess.
He really is a pest,
Even though he is bad,
And very, very mad,
I still love him very much,
I hope he loves me too.

Lottie Woolner (10)
St Catherine's RC Primary School, Bridport

Galactic Space

Space is a wonderful thing,
Stars shine like your nanny's bling bling.
As a poet I'm teaching you a lesson,
Don't mess with space or you'll have a star for your face!
Astronauts like the stars,
They want to live on Mars,
Black holes are worse than moles,
They suck up high and low.
As the sun burns terrible heat
We'll get sunburnt on our feet!

Ned Parmiter (10)
St Catherine's RC Primary School, Bridport

The Sea

The sea is brilliant, fantastic, and fun,
Its relaxing blue shimmers in the dazzling sun.

The sea is wild, exciting to see,
It's interesting to watch the waves roam free.

The sea has hypnotic and wonderful ways,
Its magical white horses surfing the bays.

But although the sea looks and acts wild and free,
It never disobeys the mighty moon.

Katherine Crabb (10)
St Catherine's RC Primary School, Bridport

Football

I try and kick the ball but all I do is fall!
I need a strike so everyone
Will like me.
I call my friends,
'Am I doing OK?'
But hey, at least I
Played for a day!

Harriet Stanley (10)
St Catherine's RC Primary School, Bridport

Rock Pooling

Rock pooling is so much fun,
Seeing the crabs lying in the sun,
Seeing the little fish swim by,
Wiggling their little fins they try,
On the rocks the starfish stick,
While the seaweed we try to pick.

Gabrielle Horton (10)
St Catherine's RC Primary School, Bridport

Space

It took a lot of haste
To reach this dark, dark place,
Where stars are gleaming,
And where planets are dreaming
Because of their own great soul.

They're both gentle,
They don't hurt,
They take it easy,
They all have friends
And family,
The planets as a nine!

Phillippa Gatehouse (9)
St Catherine's RC Primary School, Bridport

By The Sea

Hear the waves
Crashing against the sand.
See the sea
Hurrying up the land.
Look at the pebble
Lying there, getting swept away.
Listen to the echoing,
While we are all at play.
Look above your head,
See the seagulls flying in a flock.
Listen to the roaring sea.

Rosemary Shearman (9)
St Catherine's RC Primary School, Bridport

Brentford Bees

Martin Allen leads them out
All the fans jumping about
The red and whites are playing at the top
Martin saved them from the drop
The Brentford Bees are lifting their game
They've been scoring all day
Come on this is child's play
Then the final whistle blows
The Bees are victorious!

Thomas Grogan (9)
St Catherine's RC Primary School, Bridport

Aliens

Aliens, they live in space,
Flying around in a UFO
Abducting humans at a pace,
Using their eerie green glow
To attract.
They're always on the go
And they're feared, that's a fact.

Edward Whitehead (10)
St Catherine's RC Primary School, Bridport

Art!

Art is colourful,
Fun, exciting,
Draw a picture!
Paint a scene!
Make a model,
Use messy clay,
Create a collage
In a magical way!

Alice Budden (9)
St Catherine's RC Primary School, Bridport

Happiness

Happiness is like the colour blue.
It feels like a field of butterflies.
It smells like honey.
It looks like playful children.
It sounds like friends calling me.
It tastes like a lollipop.
It reminds me of fun.

Zaccarie Tregarthen-Riley (7)
St Catherine's RC Primary School, Littlehampton

Happiness

Happiness is pink like a heart floating around
It looks like romance
It tastes like chips
It feels like a tickle
It sounds like a lot of noise
It smells like a page in a new book
It reminds me of love.

Katie McIlwain (8)
St Catherine's RC Primary School, Littlehampton

Anger

Anger is like boiling hot tomato
It feels like extreme lava
It smells like horrible gas
It reminds me of my mum and dad shouting,
It looks like a red chilli,
It sounds like people crying and screaming.

Michelle Solomon (8)
St Catherine's RC Primary School, Littlehampton

Fear

Fear is black like the darkness at night
It tastes like burnt brown sausages.
It looks like smoke from a chimney.
It reminds me of scared people.
It sounds like quietness all around.
It feels like someone getting hurt.
It smells like rotten apples.

Melanie Martin (8)
St Catherine's RC Primary School, Littlehampton

Happiness

Happiness is yellow like sunflowers.
It smells like apple trees.
It sounds like friends laughing.
It tastes like gammon and hot dogs.
It feels like good times with my brother.
It looks like my friends playing.
It reminds me of my dad and mum telling me jokes.

Michael Dorey (8)
St Catherine's RC Primary School, Littlehampton

Sadness

Sadness is white like snow in the Arctic circle,
It feels like a freezing penguin in a freezer,
It sounds like a weeping door in the night,
It looks like I have a broken heart,
It tastes like a tear dropping in my mouth,
It smells like burnt toast in a toaster,
It reminds me of my homework.

Daniel Burdfield (8)
St Catherine's RC Primary School, Littlehampton

Fear

Fear is the colours grey and black.
It tastes like a spiderweb.
It smells like thick black smoke
It sounds like a wolf howling in the middle of the night.
It looks like a wolf chasing me.
It feels like a spider walking up my back.
It reminds me of a spider on my head.

Sean Ayling (8)
St Catherine's RC Primary School, Littlehampton

Silence

Silence is grey like a tiny mouse.
It smells like dirty mud.
It tastes like crisps with no flavour.
It sounds like nothingness.
It looks like blank, white everywhere.
It feels like I'm grabbing air.
It reminds me of quiet reading.

Archie Mustow (8)
St Catherine's RC Primary School, Littlehampton

Hate

Hate is grey like heavy clouds
It looks like a madman.
It smells like a pile of ashes
It tastes like carrots
It feels like fire in the wind
It sounds like a long scream
It reminds me of the Devil.

Jake Davies (8)
St Catherine's RC Primary School, Littlehampton

Love

Love is red like a rose
It sounds like a heart beating
It smells like melted chocolate
It tastes like a chocolate heart
It looks like a rose petal
It feels like a fluffy rabbit
It reminds me of my mum.

Hana-Lina Kasujja (8)
St Catherine's RC Primary School, Littlehampton

Sadness

Sadness is white like freezing snow.
It looks like a lonely child crying.
It sounds like a pack of wolves howling.
It tastes like salty sea water.
It feels like water running down your cheeks.
It smells like burning smoke.
It reminds me of rain.

Abigail Blondell (8)
St Catherine's RC Primary School, Littlehampton

Hate

Hate is grey like blasting smoke.
It reminds me of my friends not liking me.
It smells like burning fire.
It tastes bitter like a lemon.
It feels like lava erupting in my tummy.
It sounds like a man screaming in my head.
It looks like smoky spirits.

Braden Kenny (8)
St Catherine's RC Primary School, Littlehampton

Love

Love is red like a little rose.
It looks like a heart beating.
It tastes like a white heart chocolate.
It sounds like a robin tweeting.
It feels like a butterfly in my tummy.
It smells like bluebells,
It reminds me of Valentine's Day.

Siobhan Maysey (8)
St Catherine's RC Primary School, Littlehampton

Love

Love is red like a little rose.
It sounds like people singing.
It feels like dancing.
It looks like butterflies playing
It tastes like white chocolate
It reminds me of my mum kissing me goodnight.

Lucie Derrick (8)
St Catherine's RC Primary School, Littlehampton

Happiness

Happiness is like the taste of buttery bread,
Happiness is a new pet, like feeling excited,
Happiness is glowing like the shining sun
Happiness is an ice cream van chiming on a hot day
Happiness is eggs, like in a tasty sandwich.

Brittany Wilson (7)
Salmestone Primary School, Margate

Ye Olde Dragon

I'll take you back many a year,
When a popular drink wasn't invented, beer.

An olde dragon,
Once ate a supply wagon,
With all the people in despair,
The village was in disrepair.

Then a brave knight
Rode in on a bike,
He drew out his sword,
He jumped on a wooden board,
He soared in the air,
In the wind, he lost his underwear.

He cut the humungous throat of the dragon,
And out of the body flew the old wagon,
If it wasn't for Saint George's bam and a bim
If he did run away, we wouldn't blame him

I'll take you back many a year,
When a popular drink wasn't invented, beer.

Tom Harman (9)
Sibertswold CE Primary School, Shepherdswell

Guess Who?

He's as clean as a car
He's as sharp as a knife
He's as bouncy as a kangaroo,
He's as strong as a gorilla
He's as fast as a Formula 1 racer,
He's as fierce as a jaguar.

He is Alexi!

Jacob Roberts (8)
Sibertswold CE Primary School, Shepherdswell

Seasons

Spring is always full of joy
Spring is always full of hope
Spring is always full of peace
Spring is always full of sunshine.

Summer is always full of fun
Summer is always full of happiness
Summer is always full of love
Summer is always full of sky and sun.

Autumn is always full of kindness
Autumn is always full of happy children
Autumn is always full of helpfulness
Autumn is always full of brown leaves falling off trees.

Winter is always full of warm log fires
Winter is always full of sheets of white snow
Winter is always full of bare trees
Winter is always full of white snow.

Ruby Russell (9)
Sibertswold CE Primary School, Shepherdswell

Ghost, Mr Ghost

In my bedroom there's a ghost,
I call him Mr Ghost
He always comes to play with me
When he comes out he should stay with me,
But back in he goes.

But when it's summer he never plays again
And I call him Mr Ghost
Soon he will live and give
And be able to fly in the sky.

Brandon Forrest (8)
Sibertswold CE Primary School, Shepherdswell

What Are We Made Of?

What are our mums made of?
What are our mums made of?
Robots which care
And are always there,
That's what our mums are made of.

What are our dads made of?
What are our dads made of?
Sticks and stones
And lots of bones,
That's what our dads are made of.

What are our brothers made of?
What are our brothers made of?
People that fight
And sometimes bite,
That's what our brothers are made of.

What are our sisters made of?
What are our sisters made of?
Kids that are funky
But act like a monkey,
That's what our sisters are made of.

What are we made of?
What are we made of?
Lots of fun
But no pieces of dumb,
That's what we are made of.

Annabel Reville (9)
Sibertswold CE Primary School, Shepherdswell

Funny Farm

There was a duck
They called him Chuck
He took a shower
And turned into a flower.

There was a cat
Who wore a hat,
Sat on a mat
And turned into a rat.

There was a fox
Who got chickenpox,
Fell down a well
And turned into a bell.

There was a lion
Who liked to eat iron,
Touched a nettle,
And turned to metal.

Alex Hamby (9)
Sibertswold CE Primary School, Shepherdswell

The Wild

In the wild there are animals,
The animals are nice, the deer are sweet and calm,
The foxes protect,
The moles live blind,
There are plants and trees in the woods,
The trees get destroyed.

In the wild they make more animals together,
The features are natural,
In the wild, the wild horses are on the road,
The wild is good,
It is nature,
All of the trees get destroyed,
By the woodcutters.

Charlotte Powell (9)
Sibertswold CE Primary School, Shepherdswell

Stingray

Stingray, stingray,
He's coming, hooray,
He's cutting through the water to save the day.
He meets lots of fish on his way,
They don't even bother to say, 'Good day.'

He goes to the postman and says, 'Any post?'
The postman says, 'Yes, straight from the coast.'
He opens the letter and it's from Aunty Netter.

He sees a boat,
That is afloat,
But sinking fast,
So you can't see the mast.

Stingray, stingray,
He's coming, hooray,
He's cutting through the water to save the day.

Claire Penny (8)
Sibertswold CE Primary School, Shepherdswell

My Cat

My cat is a fat cat, slobby cat, he eats too much!
He sleeps during the day and is awake at night, what a funny cat:
He purrs when you stroke him, nice and gentle,
But other than that, he's a fat funny cat,
He's a cute cat, but very lazy, except when you call him for tea!
He loves the summer and plays with me, all day long.
When it's time for lunch, he'll follow me, munch, munch!

And that's my fat cat!
Oh! Shh! He's asleep, what a surprise! Zzz!

Laura Palmer (9)
Sibertswold CE Primary School, Shepherdswell

The Rapping Poem

The teachers are cool,
Like playing pool,
The children are nice,
Like little mice.

The cats are rapping,
Rapping round,
The dogs are barking,
Rapping down to the beat of the ground.

The teachers are cool,
Like playing pool,
The children are nice
Like little mice.

The whole city is rapping to the town,
They're rapping together, with a very funny clown,
All our bodies are jiggling about,
To the rap to the slip, slap, slout rap.

Chloe Peerless (9)
Sibertswold CE Primary School, Shepherdswell

Guess Who?

He is as sharp as a knife
He is as fast as a cheetah
He is as sly as a fox
He is as strong as a sumo
He is as furry as a monkey
He is as flexible as a rubber
He is as cool as a leather jacket,

He is Harry.

Alexi Payne (9)
Sibertswold CE Primary School, Shepherdswell

Seasons

Summer

Summer is great,
There's always a fête,
Flowers are blooming,
There's always someone moving.

Winter

Winter is the season,
Where there is a reason,
There's always something strange,
With the range.

Autumn

Autumn is weird,
Like an old man's beard,
The leaves are golden brown,
They fall on the ground.

Spring

All the baby animals are born,
Yes, on the lawn,
The sun is shining,
No more mining.

Abigail McLean (9)
Sibertswold CE Primary School, Shepherdswell

Guess Who?

He is as fast as a flaming jaguar,
He is a maniac monkey,
He is as funny as a flying frog,
He is a shiny sun,
He is fun and funky.
He is my best friend, Alexi P.

Harry Moore (9)
Sibertswold CE Primary School, Shepherdswell

I Wish I Were . . .

I wish I were a racing car,
Speeding down the roads.
I wish I were an aeroplane,
Whizzing through the clouds,
I wish I were a stingray swimming in the sea.

I wish I were a sparrowhawk,
Swooping up and down.
I wish I were a British jet
Bombing all the towns.
I wish I were a satsuma,
Best of all the fruit.
I wish I were a woodpecker
Pecking all the trees.

George Fordham (9)
Sibertswold CE Primary School, Shepherdswell

The Cool Poem

He's as cool as a banana,
He's as cool as a pool
He's as great as a gate
He's as nice as ice
He's as good as gold
He's as smart as a tart,
He's as mean as a machine,
He's as fierce as a tiger
He's as cool as, *stop!*
He's Harry!

Nicholas Dray (9)
Sibertswold CE Primary School, Shepherdswell

Horses!

The pony came out of the stable door,
It walked for a while then stood on the floor,
He heard all the birds singing a nice little song,
But he saw his friends ahead and cantered on.

He played with his friends till late at night
And carried on till morning light.
He went to his stable to have some nice food,
After that he was in a very good mood.

He went into the field to have a ride,
But of course his friend was by his side.
He went really fast out to the field,
He went really fast you would think he was skilled!

Lucy Gilchrist (9)
Sibertswold CE Primary School, Shepherdswell

The World

The world is big, it used to be empty
Now there are lots of countries,
In those countries there are things,
Things like trees, things like bees.
There are animals far and wide,
Small ones, tall ones and cool ones.
People go to shops, huge ones I say,
We like everything in this world,
We like the dogs, the cats and the sea,
We see, we like, everything in this world.

Alice Heath (10)
Sibertswold CE Primary School, Shepherdswell

My Skeleton

This is my poem about my skeleton,
I called him Mickal Eleton.
I'm called Moe,
And this is his toe,
My last name is Palm,
And this is his arm.
This is a skeleton, can you see?
He goes flip, flop, tip, tap, wee!

The bones are dull,
And this is his skull,
Its got lips, eyes and ears and some tears
This is a skeleton, can you see?
He goes flip, flop, tip, tap, wee!

Laura Castledine (8)
Sibertswold CE Primary School, Shepherdswell

The Fantastic Mixable Poem

My friend is a pain,
According to his name.
My uncle calls me Puke,
But my real name is Luke.
My sisters are pains,
Just like bumpy lanes.

Tom is a bomb,
Just like Dick and Dom.
My brother's fat,
Just like a big bat.
I am smelly,
And I like jelly.

Luke Firth-Coppock (9)
Sibertswold CE Primary School, Shepherdswell

My Favourite Food

I love chips,
I don't eat pips,
I hate mustard,
And I'm not too keen on custard,
I like to pig out on my favourite food,
I don't like nasty and I don't do rude!

I hate the taste of banana,
And my sister is a nana,
I like orange juice,
And I don't like lemon mousse,
I like to pig out on my favourite food,
I don't like nasty and I don't do rude!

I love the taste of apple,
I would eat it in a chapel,
I love chicken pie,
And I won't tell a lie,
I like to pig out on my favourite food,
I don't like nasty and I don't do rude!

Hannah Coupe (8)
Sibertswold CE Primary School, Shepherdswell

Shapes

She's as round as a circle,
She's as pointy as a square,
She's as sharp as a triangle,
She's as clever as a rectangle,
She's as big as a cube,
She's as kind as a cone.

Who is she?
My best friend!

Shannah Hall (9)
Sibertswold CE Primary School, Shepherdswell

Guess Who?

She's as tall as the London Eye,
She's as snug as a blanket,
She's as cool as a jaguar,
She's as pretty as a poppy,
She's as precious as a diamond,
      She's Mrs Ashcroft.

She's as small as an ant,
She's as cute as a teddy,
She's as fun as a bike,
She's as shiny as a ring,
She's as cuddly as a rabbit,
      She's Hannah.

She's as fast as a cheetah,
She's as fun as a computer,
She's as cool as an ice cube,
She's as hard as a rock,
She's as bouncy as a trampoline,
      She's Lucy.

She's as sweet as a lemon,
She's as funny as a hyena,
She's as soft as a pillow,
She's as cool as an ice lolly,
She's as smart as an owl.
      She's Mrs Ardley.

Molly Billington (8)
Sibertswold CE Primary School, Shepherdswell

The Family Poem

My dog is as cool
As a football,
My dog is no fool.

My sister is as dumb
As my thumb,
My dad is as tall as a wall.

I love my mum
She's not dumb,
My cousin Tom is a bomb,
Just like Dick and Dom.

Brandon Faulkner (9)
Sibertswold CE Primary School, Shepherdswell

Volcano Pompeii AD 79

The volcano explodes with a bang,
Everyone is still.
Suddenly it belts layers of ash
Over the small town.
The people run screaming
With fright and in fear.
Homes fall crumbling.
Layers of ash
Grow higher and bigger.
More screaming and running.
Animals squealing
Not knowing what to do.
Total confusion.
Buildings thundering down
On all the stricken and helpless.
The town of Pompeii was no more . . .

. . . until it was
Discovered again.

Max Brown (10)
South Stoke Primary School, South Stoke

Battlefield Sounds

The soldier and his rifle,
Crunching sand under heavy boots.

Machine gun ricocheting off stone
Stuttering, a splitting noise of ice.

Whizzing bullets, cries of the helpless
Wounded in the midst of battle.

Shells, thundering rockets
Whistling, falling through the sky
Tanks creating terrifying explosions.

Help at last sobbing men, crying with relief.
Sounds of victory ringing through the streets, on and on.

George Scholey (11)
South Stoke Primary School, South Stoke

Fear

Fear is black
Like a dark room.

It sounds like wind
Blowing through trees.

It smells like ice
And tastes of rotten fruit.

Fear is horrible.

Eloise Craven-Todd (11)
South Stoke Primary School, South Stoke

Sadness

Sadness is the softest violet,
Hailstones clattering are the sound of sadness,
Sadness feels hard in my hands and smells like a garden,
Flowers in the spring might taste of sadness.

Kimberley Ambler (11)
South Stoke Primary School, South Stoke

Disco Sounds From The 'Amarillo Centre'

Drums beating out loud music
For everyone to hear,
Big boys beating up
Little girls and boys,
The bouncer dragging out the drunk
Into the street,
The laughter.

Strings breaking on guitars,
People crying,
Loving the music.
Wine glasses shattering
On the floor,
The sobbing.

People eating and
Shouting for refills.
Money dropping,
Scavengers picking it up
And pocketing it,
The laughter.
The sobbing.

Oliver Craven-Todd (9)
South Stoke Primary School, South Stoke

Beach Sounds At Weston-Super-Mare

Ice cream vans playing their music encourage people to buy
The echoes of amusements on the pier,
Children screaming as they jump into the waves,
Boats zooming past just like motorbikes,
Sounds from radios belting through town
The sea whooshing into rocks, wind howling like wolves,
Weston-super-Mare.

Grace Beacham-Vickery (11)
South Stoke Primary School, South Stoke

Happiness

Happiness is green
Like grass in the fields.
It sounds like birds singing
In a sunny breeze.
If I could touch happiness
It would feel like you
Standing right beside me.

Joseph Kitt (10)
South Stoke Primary School, South Stoke

Love

Love is like the glowing moon
It is tenderness
Yet with the uncertainty of a shadow
And so gentle, a fluffy soft bed
Love is kind and understanding
Sometimes sad and disappointing
Love is a friend.

Scott Harwood (10)
South Stoke Primary School, South Stoke

Fear

Fear is black ink
Sounding like shock
A solid block of shouting
The smell of a wet tree
And taste on my tongue
Hot, black, fire ashes.

Rebecca Stevens (10)
South Stoke Primary School, South Stoke

The Mosque

The ringing bell flows in the air
Marking the start of the day.
The sound of Koran's turning pages
Echoes all around the space.
The chanting of people
Like a war cry.
Silence disrupted only by
Flapping of birds in the tower.
Feet resounding like marble smashing
Into a million pieces
On the cold marble floor.
Quiet broken,
A chorus of bells
Chiming in rhythm.
Prayer.

Harry Haslam (11)
South Stoke Primary School, South Stoke

I Could Be . . .

(Based on 'The You Can Be ABC' by Roger Stevens)

I could be a
Terrible teacher or a fuzzy footballer
A worldwide weather woman or a nutty nanny
A disco dancer or a crazy cook
A bossy bus driver or a spectacular swordsman
An artistic artist or a moaning musician
An optimistic opera singer or a junior juggler
A groovy girl or a pop star policeman.

Georgia Stevenson (8)
Spinners Acre Junior School, Chatham

I Could Be . . .

(Based on 'The You Can Be ABC' by Roger Stevens)

I could be an angry ancestor or a beastly bus driver
A crazy conductor or a dizzy daddy
An envoy enemy or a funny footballer
A gruesome ghost or a heroic hero
An international inventor or a junior juggler
A kicking king or a lurking labourer
A monstrous musician or a nutty nanny
An obnoxious optician or a paralysing poet
A queasy queen or a reckless rider
A spectacular swordsman or a terrible teacher
A useless undertaker or a valiant vet
A wonderful worker or an X-raying X-ray bird
A yummy yellow yacht or a ziggy zaggy zookeeper.

Ryan Catt (8)
Spinners Acre Junior School, Chatham

I Could Be . . .

(Based on 'The You Can Be ABC' by Roger Stevens)

I could be an angry actor or a bad bus driver
A crafty cook or a dizzy doctor
An electric electrician or a fatty footballer
A great garbage man or a jolly juggler
A loppy lollipop lady or a killer karate teacher
A mad mockingbird or a knitting nanny
A professional pop star or a super spy
A terrible truck driver or a reckless rider
A useless undertaker or a kung-fu kangaroo.

Connor Preston (8)
Spinners Acre Junior School, Chatham

I Could Be . . .

(Based on 'The You Can Be ABC' by Roger Stevens)

I could be
A silly sister or a fantastic friend
An angry artist or a dizzy daydreamer
A beautiful ballerina or a crazy car driver
A missing mermaid or a nailing nanny
A terrible teacher or a popping pop star
A lovely leader or a quizzing queen.

Ella Quinn (8)
Spinners Acre Junior School, Chatham

I Could Be . . .

(Based on 'The You Can Be ABC' by Roger Stevens)

A terrible train driver or a nice nanny
A dirty dancer or a silly singer
A loopy Lauren or a famous friend
A jolly juggler or a beautiful ballerina
An evil enemy or a wonderful winner.

Lauren Breach (8)
Spinners Acre Junior School, Chatham

I Could Be . . .

(Based on 'The You Can Be ABC' by Roger Stevens)

I could be an angry Amiee or a beautiful ballerina
A clever child or a dirty dentist
A fantasy dress-up person or a loopy Lauren
A crazy cook or a terrible teacher
A dangerous doctor or a miserable mum.

Amiee Fowle (8)
Spinners Acre Junior School, Chatham

I Could Be . . .

(Based on 'The You Can Be ABC' by Roger Stevens)

I could be
An arty artist or a beautiful ballet dancer
A crazy cook or a dizzy dancer
A fussy footballer or a naughty nanny
An over-the-top opera singer or a zany zookeeper
A popping pop star or a hairy hairdresser
An unhappy umpire or a moaning mum
An evil enemy or a rotting rat
A green garden or a terrifying teacher.

Hannah Eldridge (8)
Spinners Acre Junior School, Chatham

I Could Be . . .

(Based on 'The You Can Be ABC' by Roger Stevens)

I could be
A talented train driver or a reckless rider
A monstrous musician or a funny footballer
A nutty nanny or a crazy car driver
A junior juggler or a quippy quiz-master
A serious scientist or a handsome hippo.

Joe Chaney (8)
Spinners Acre Junior School, Chatham

I Could Be . . .

(Based on 'The You Can Be ABC' by Roger Stevens)

I could be a beautiful ballerina or a terrific train driver
A naughty nanny or a silly sister
A fantastic footballer or a duelling joker
A crazy cat or a fantastic fish.

Olivia Watters (8)
Spinners Acre Junior School, Chatham

I Could Be . . .

(Based on 'The You Can Be ABC' by Roger Stevens)

I could be
An angry actor or a bad boy
A crazy car driver or a dribbly dad
An evil elf or a fat father
A giggling girl or a handsome hippopotamus
A nutty nan or a super sister
A mad mummy or a lazy lady.

Joshua Boyce (8)
Spinners Acre Junior School, Chatham

A Hunting Dog

I'm a hunting dog,
I hear gun dogs all the time.
I listen to *my* master,
I love him really.

I can see people beating
Pheasants falling from the sky
Dogs running around . . . *'Come Duster!'*
My turn.

I can feel the earth beneath my feet
The pheasant in my mouth,
The blood trickling down my neck
I can feel my master taking it out of my mouth
And him patting me on my head.

I can smell pheasant's blood and people
I can almost smell them cooking
But I don't get given scraps because it's not for dogs
I can also smell different smells, rats, foxes and badgers.

Kate Butler (10)
Sticklands VA Primary School, Evershot

World War II

I am a soldier in World War II
Along with millions of soldiers,
All around me I can see,
Along with millions of soldiers,
People running with the flu,
Along with millions of soldiers,
There are planes flying high.

Bombs being dropped,
Along with millions of soldiers,
Scared mothers and their children,
Along with millions of soldiers,
By a siren silence stopped,
Along with millions of soldiers,
German soldiers docking ships.

Inside I know I will die,
Along with millions of soldiers,
And go to Heaven up high,
Along with millions of soldiers,
I am in the ambulance,
Along with five other soldiers.

I am in the hospital,
Along with millions of soldiers,
I am dying, I can't breathe well,
Along with millions of soldiers,
I am dead, silent and dead,
Along with millions of soldiers.

Jasmine Anstey (10)
Sticklands VA Primary School, Evershot

On The Bus

On the bus
I could see the sun shining in the sky,
In front of me I could see all the children,
I could hear hands clapping together
The engine hunting up the hill
The bus stopping to pick someone up, people chattering
Here I am at school,
I'm happy playing with my friends.

Ryan Edmonds (10)
Sticklands VA Primary School, Evershot

Hate

Hate is orange like a roaring light,
It sounds like a screaming ball
Screaming through the night.
It tastes like a hot pepperoni burning in the mouth
It smells like a burning cigarette letting out gas
It looks like fire burning in the eye,
It feels like your organs twisting and turning in your tummy,
It reminds me of the ashes of a burning fire.

Jack Harvey (10)
Sticklands VA Primary School, Evershot

Anger

Anger is black like a stormy day.
Anger sounds like an earthquake destroying cities,
Anger tastes like bitter lemon juice,
Anger smells like fumes from a car in a polluted city,
Anger looks like a ring of fire.
Anger feels like a block of hard coal,
It reminds me of being beaten up.

George Hile (9)
Sticklands VA Primary School, Evershot

What Am I?

Water-splasher,
No-wheeler
Engine-revver
Water-glider
Speed-flasher,
Diesel-drinker
Motor-racer,
Easy-rider,
Time-setter,
Light-pacer,
What am I?

A speedboat!

Lee Edwards (10)
Sticklands VA Primary School, Evershot

What Am I?

Penalty taker
Hacking faker
Free kicker
Great tricker
Ref waiter
See you later
Ball hogger
Posh snogger
Ball whacker
Great cracker
Good hammer
What a slammer.

Alex Gordon (10)
Sticklands VA Primary School, Evershot

Boris' Big Scare

I am Boris the forest mouse,
My enemies are grey snakes,
I've got a hole; it's my house,
Around it are three lakes,

One dark morning the moment came,
I was face to face with a snake,
It didn't help since my foot was lame,
The claws looked like a rake,

All I could hear was the sound of its tongue,
I was feeling really frightened,
The feeling made my body feel stung,
The sun came out and the area lightened,

The sun was so bright the snake went away,
Leaving behind its channel-like trail,
In relief I shouted, 'Hooray!'
It's just lucky the snake wasn't a male!

Christopher James (11)
Sticklands VA Primary School, Evershot

Silence

Silence is white and clear,
Silence is white and clear like a quiet cloud,
Silence is white and clear and sounds like an empty room,
Silence is white and clear and it tastes like cold, raw meat,
Silence is white and clear and smells like a damp, empty church,
Silence is white and clear and looks like an empty cardboard box,
Silence is white and clear and feels like a smooth wall,
It reminds me of a deserted railway yard.

Oliver Wells (10)
Sticklands VA Primary School, Evershot

What Am I?

Tail-wagger
Cat-tagger.

Good-sniffer,
Nose-wiffer.

Rabbit-crazy,
Rather-lazy.

Tongue-hanger,
Bad-tanger.

Begging-eyes,
Mournful-cries.

What am I?

Jessica Pring (9)
Sticklands VA Primary School, Evershot

Our Dog Missy

Our dog is very naughty
She's dug a great big hole
I don't know what she's looking for
Maybe it's the mole

When she's finished digging
Her paws are not so clean
So in the bath we pop her
She thinks we're being mean

We love our dog called Missy
When clean or when mucky
We wouldn't be without her
Because she is our puppy.

Cara Waite (8)
Stoke Poges School, Stoke Poges

Playground Problems

Miss! Miss! Come, come quick!
Sarah's stuck and
Tangled in twigs!

Miss! Miss! Hurry up now!
Jen ripped her tights and
Has torn her blouse!

Miss! Miss! Don't waste time!
Joe let the parrot out and
Don't you mind?

Miss! Miss! You're taking too long!
Mickey dyed her hair and
Got it all wrong!

Miss! Miss! The playground's a disaster!
Children are on the streets and
The school is on *fire!*

Malaika Kingue (10)
Stoke Poges School, Stoke Poges

Water, Water Everywhere!

Water, water everywhere
Water, water it's not rare
Water, water in your bath
Water, water makes you laugh
Water, water you can drink
Water, water in your sink
Water, water to clean your dishes
Water, for my pet fishes
Water is a helpful source
I love water (of course).

Aman Dhillon (8)
Stoke Poges School, Stoke Poges

Skiing

When I go down a hill
As fast as I can,
I feel scared and frightened.
I feel like I'm going to fall forward.
Sometimes I feel excited,
And it can be fun.
It's a lot of pain,
With the cold rushing past my face.
But it can be fun skiing.

Naveen Mahil (8)
Stoke Poges School, Stoke Poges

Cats

A cat has lovely soft paws
It purrs when he or she is happy,
Cats are sweet and soft too
Some are fat, some are thin,
But my cat is just right,
And I love him so much!

Sophia Young (8)
Stoke Poges School, Stoke Poges

The Little Bear

If you see the dangling little bear
Make sure he is welcomed,
He's got brown fur and blue eyes,
He likes cuddling up with you at night,
He looks fierce, but he's like a baby inside.

Emma Calnan (10)
Stoke Poges School, Stoke Poges

Dolphins

Dolphins always like to play
There they could stay
For all of the day.
The bottlenose
Is on TV shows
Dolphins communicate with clicks,
Tame dolphins learn many tricks,
Dolphins have sharp teeth
And swim in and out of the reef
Most dolphins in the north
Love to swim of course.
All dolphins eat fish
And if I had just one wish
It would be to swim and dive
And with the dolphins I'd have a ride.

Bethan Nankivell (9)
Stoke Poges School, Stoke Poges

The Beach

The sea is cold and calm
The waves are shining and are crystal clear
As they roll onto the golden sand.
The palm trees are swaying from side to side
The children running and screaming across the hot sand
Adults relaxing peacefully on the deckchairs
The creatures in the sea, mostly fish
I really do wish.

Simran Gill (8)
Stoke Poges School, Stoke Poges

What Am I?

I come before lightning,
I follow the rain,
I make windows rattle,
I can shake the windowpane.

I can scare little children
And terrifying their pets.
I can roar like a lion,
I can injure jumbo jets.

If I'm mean please take cover,
I can blow you away
What's the point of umbrellas
If I'm coming your way?

I disturb seas and lakes
And tease the little streams,
I boss my brother lightning
And laugh at the sun's beams

I'm mightier than the wind
I cover the weak sky,
I am better than lightning,
So which force am I?

Sasha Jhalli (11)
Stoke Poges School, Stoke Poges

Thundery Nights

Thundery nights knock down the trees,
Thundery nights scare the bees,
Thunder snaps the pylon wires,
Thunder causes loads of fires,
Thunder makes a crashing noise,
Thunder scares the girls and boys.

Luke (9)
Stoke Poges School, Stoke Poges

Mother Nature

Thank you Mother Nature, thank you
For colours bright and new,
Gold, pink and even blue,
Spring, summer, autumn and winter
Are seasons of the year,
Sometimes hot and sometimes cold,
But it doesn't worry me here.

Look at the beauty in the trees
With all the multicoloured leaves.
I am amazed by what I see,
Lucky, lucky, lucky me.

Just listen to the voices of the birds,
The best singing I have ever heard.
Beautiful choruses morning and night,
Some with colours beautiful and bright.

Nicole Smith (11)
Stoke Poges School, Stoke Poges

Football Crazy

I'm football crazy,
I'm football mad,
I love football,
So does my dad.
We play in the morning,
We play at night.
To get me in is quite a fight,
So when I go to sleep tonight
I'll dream and dream of being a football star
'Alright!'

Casey Rhodes (8)
Stoke Poges School, Stoke Poges

Guess My Pets

My pets are wonderful,
My pets are nice,
Except for when,
They catch some mice.

My pets are cute,
Playful too,
Leave them in privacy,
When they're in the loo.

Do you know?
Can you guess
What kind of pets I have?
Is it a cat?
Is it a dog?
Or is it a snake?

Ben Lathrope (8)
Stoke Poges School, Stoke Poges

The Crocodile Song

Neither spots nor stripes have I,
But I have beautiful green scales.
And I have
Jaws, jaws, jaws.

Neither horns nor wings have I,
But I crawl across the mud,
And I have
Jaws, jaws, jaws.

I master every movement
For I can run, jump, swim.
And I have
Jaws, jaws, jaws.

Rabiah Khalid (10)
Stoke Poges School, Stoke Poges

War

Through the day,
Throughout the night,
Soldiers march into the fight,
Bullets flying from those guns,
Some of which will kill our sons,
Such a waste of human lives,
Making widows of their wives,
Mr Blair it isn't right,
Please bring them back on the next flight!

Jordan Palmer (8)
Stoke Poges School, Stoke Poges

Skiing

I'm going down the mountain
I really can't stop
I'm definitely going to fall
Especially from the top!

I've finally found how to do it
It's still very cold
I feel like I'm flying
But I really don't want to go!

Aneesha Mahil (10)
Stoke Poges School, Stoke Poges

There Was A Young Boy . . .

There was a young boy called Freddie,
Who always cuddled his teddy.
He wetted his bed,
Which soaked poor old Ted.
That leaky young boy called Freddie.

Demi (10)
Stoke Poges School, Stoke Poges

In The Playground

In the playground is where kids have fun and a run,
They kick the ball and have a fall,
They play rope skipping and ball.

There are sometimes tears but mostly joy,
That's what happens when you mix girls and boys.

It does not matter, rain or shine,
Life in the playground is always just fine.

Taylor Nelmes (8)
Stoke Poges School, Stoke Poges

Friends

Friends are the best,
Not just in the west
But everywhere
I have lots
More than a thousand pots
They stick up for you
I have more than ten women and men
I like my friends.

Lewis Howell (8)
Stoke Poges School, Stoke Poges

June Morning - Cinquain

Morning
Birds chirping tunes
Like a choir's singing
On a lovely sunny morning
In June.

Sarah Dormand (10)
Stoke Poges School, Stoke Poges

Summer's Playground

On a warm, sticky summer's day,
Me and my friends would like to play.
But we lie on the grass,
As the butterflies fly past.
We make daisy chains for each other
But we love to make one for our mother.
The sound of the whistle touches our ears,
Slowly we walk to the line-up with our peers.
We leave the summer's day
And go our way.

Ayesha Mahmood (9)
Stoke Poges School, Stoke Poges

Spring

When you go out into my back garden
There are lots of bushes and trees in it.
There are millions of leaves in there too
And flowers as well.
When it's windy you can hear
All the leaves rustle with the wind.
When it's warm we have barbecues
Till late on the weekends.

Alisha Panue (9)
Stoke Poges School, Stoke Poges

There Was An Old Man From Dublin

There was an old man from Dublin
Who on his big feet wore a tin
He had a pet rabbit
Who hopped for a habit
That stupid old man from Dublin.

Jack Waite (11)
Stoke Poges School, Stoke Poges

Boa Constrictor Kennings

A mad crusher
A rodent eater

A whole-egg swallower
A tail body

A bird catcher
A long fang

A heavy weight
A forked tongue

A sharp sighter
A worm's cousin

A swift eater
A bone masher.

Henry Warren (11)
Stoke Poges School, Stoke Poges

What Am I? Kennings

Bone scoffer
Cat chaser

Noisy barker
Furry sniffer

Joyful walker
Fast runner

Angry biter
Tail wager

Attention lover
Scruffy troublemaker.

Lucy Smith (11)
Stoke Poges School, Stoke Poges

The Rabbit Song

Neither horns nor hooves have I,
But I have a bushy tail
And I leap, leap, leap,
Neither slime nor scales have I,
But I live in a warren
And I leap, leap, leap,
I master every movement
For I leap, hop and dodge
And I leap, leap, leap!

Anagha Sharma (8)
Stoke Poges School, Stoke Poges

The Dragon

Scaly wanderer,
Fiery breath, bat-like wings
The mythical king.

Soaring through the sky,
A purple streak in the night
Eagles by his side.

He gives a loud roar,
Fire bursts from between his jaws,
He raises his claws.

There is more here,
Unicorns play in the woods,
Centaurs galloping.

The dragon watches
As together they gather
He has called them all.

Oonagh Fox (10)
Stourfield Junior School, Bournemouth

Brothers

B rothers, brothers 4 of them
R ioting all the time
O beying nothing Mum says to them
T ug of war getting silly
H appy but they're quite a bore
E ating everything they can see
R unning away from any chore
S ometimes I can't believe they're my brothers.

Lucy Pennick (11)
Stourfield Junior School, Bournemouth

Star Wars

Spaceships flying everywhere,
Transport out of this world,
Anakin is Darth Vader,
Robot hand has Darth Vader,
Wars in every film,
Anakin's son is Luke Skywalker,
Raging with a light sabre,
Sith is evil.

Alexander Travis (10)
Stourfield Junior School, Bournemouth

Magic World

Flying through a world of magic,
Where the heavens open up and stare,
Walking on an invisible path,
Where freedom is ahead,
Looking at the rise of colour,
As the heavens sprinkle down,
Loving the nature that surrounds us.

Alice Brown (11)
Stourfield Junior School, Bournemouth

Rabbit

Carrot cruncher
Lettuce muncher

Fur scratcher
Grass snatcher

Cage creeper
Cute sleeper

Flea itcher
Nose twitcher

Tail bopper
Body hopper
Tummy flopper.

Lydia Smith (11)
Stourfield Junior School, Bournemouth

White Labrador

Paw-padder
Patting-lover
Stone-chomper
Sudden-leaper
Cat-chaser
Creamy-colour
Human-horror
Big-eater
Fast-runner
Tail-wagger.

Sarah Kearsey (10)
Stourfield Junior School, Bournemouth

Cat

There is a cat called Trevor
AKA Mary-weather
He ran down the stairs,
Wearing long flares
He doesn't frighten me
I'll just have him for tea
And I'll lean on my knee
Up high in a tree
He's getting old
As I've been told.

Tom Hall (11)
Stourfield Junior School, Bournemouth

The Library

I really like the library
With lots of books to read,
There are so many different kinds of books
I wonder where to begin.
So why don't you come to the library
And pick one for yourself.

Jay Branch (12)
Stourfield Junior School, Bournemouth

The Dragon

The dragon is a female
The dragon is a reptile,
The dragon smokes,
It lives in a castle,
Knights are its favourite lunch,
It has big claws.

Jason Brown-Burt (11)
Stourfield Junior School, Bournemouth

Hamster Flake

Bear-poser
    People-lover
Wheel-runner
    Quick-scurrier
Night-awaker
    Day-sleeper
Food-lover
    Treat-adorer
Cage-chewer
    Constant-pooer.

Gregory Roy (10)
Stourfield Junior School, Bournemouth

Dog

Cat-chaser
Tail-wagger
Milk-drinker
Toy-chewer
Long-whiskers
Hole-digger
People-lover
Face-licker
Bath-hater
Bone-eater.

Benedict Petch (11)
Stourfield Junior School, Bournemouth

My Rabbit

Nose-twitcher
Ear-flinger
Head-hider
Cuddle-lover
Friend-maker
Proud-poser
Glove-chaser
High-leaper
Leaf-devourer
Carrot-guzzler.

Hannah Daykin (11)
Stourfield Junior School, Bournemouth

Chocolate

I love chocolate so much
Because it makes me happy
When I wore a nappy
It's so good to touch
Cause it melts in your hands
And my favourite flavour is white
I hope no one likes a human chocolate man.

James Diffey (11)
Stourfield Junior School, Bournemouth

Cheetah - Haiku

Black spots on the back,
Orange body on the ground,
Down low to catch prey.

Alana Strutt (10)
Stourfield Junior School, Bournemouth

Dogs

Night-stalker
Sleep-walker
Loud-barker
Brilliant-player
Ball-catcher
Food-snatcher
Teeth-rotter
Fast-runner
Tail-wagger
Ear-flopper.

Sian Scorer (11)
Stourfield Junior School, Bournemouth

Rabbits

Ground beater
Carrot eater
Skin scratcher
Food catcher
Dandelion muncher
Enemy puncher
Leaf chewer
Multiple pooer.

Ryan Galpin (11)
Stourfield Junior School, Bournemouth

Looking Out

Out of my bedroom window I look
I see the sun shining through the trees
The wind blows
It sounds like wolves howling at the moon.
As the sun sets to rest
The white sphere comes up it shines brightly
To lighten up the dark black sky.

Claudia Welcome (10)
Stourfield Junior School, Bournemouth

A New Adventure

I started my life when I left my mum,
I was only a few yards away from her.
I landed on a soft brown thing,
I couldn't move.
I could feel some more pouring on me,
It was dark and scary
I knew I was growing,
But into what?

I started growing my hair green,
And lots of legs
I turned a pale colour with spots,
I saw worms everywhere,
Snails nibbling my skin.

I had a relaxing bath,
But it was cold.
I could hear voices,
Then I saw daylight.

Something put me in a bag,
It was dark and scary
Something took me out
Put me in a small room, with other po-po-potatoes
And put me on a tall shelf,
A beginning of a new life.

Georgina Ralph (10)
Whitehill Junior School, Gravesend

Relaxing In The Garden

What can I see?
I can see the light blue sky,
The sky is very high.
With the clouds floating by.

What can I hear?
I can hear the birds singing,
Lots of their things bringing,
Children playing catch with a ball,
Against the old Victorian wall.

What can I feel?
I can feel the wind against my cheek,
I can see a little bird's yellow beak,
I feel my heart beating fast,
I think it will be the last.

Children relaxing in the garden, playing on the grass.

Shannon Firth (11)
Whitehill Junior School, Gravesend

School

He saw the children kicking the ball into the goal,
He saw children pushing through the door, up the stairs
                                    and into classroom,
He heard the teacher writing on the blackboard,
He saw the children writing in their books,
He smelt the dinners cooking in the school kitchen,
He ran upstairs to get his dinner money,
He smelt the teacher's perfume on the teacher's desk,
He smelt the air coming from the class windows,
He ran downstairs to get his dinner,
He sat in the dinner hall all alone,
He ran outside and had his play,
He had his day and went home.

Lauren Perkins (11)
Whitehill Junior School, Gravesend

Billy Joe

Hi, I am Billy Joe out of Green Day,
I am going to tell you what I can see, feel and hear in my band.

What can I see?
I see fans crowding around the gates,
I see electric guitars and drums,
Directors telling me where to stand on the stage.

What can I feel?
I feel nervous, as I'm just about to go on stage and play,
I feel great that we have started,
It feels like great fun as we rock on stage.

What can I hear?
I hear people going crazy,
People singing along with us,
Now the gig is over.

I had excellent fun hanging around talking about myself,
See you later.

Matthew Martin (10)
Whitehill Junior School, Gravesend

Feelings And Colours

Excitement is multicoloured,
Like a sparkling, glittery rainbow!

Sadness is navy blue,
Like the deepest, darkest sea.

Horror is black,
Like an endless tunnel.

Cheerfulness is peach,
Like the sun falling for a goodnight's sleep!

Love is pink,
Like candyfloss melting on my tongue.

Chloe Stannard (11)
Whitehill Junior School, Gravesend

Football Mad

Into the stadium, proud of my team

What can you see?
Football players warming-up,
Ref walking onto the pitch,
Teams shaking hands,
And the match beginning.

What can you hear?
Fans cheering loudly,
Footballers shouting for the ball,
Ref blowing his whistle,
Sound of net rattling.

What do you feel?
We are going to win,
Wind blowing,
The ball hitting me and the crowd,
The rain at full time,
Yes! We won 2-0!

Out of the stadium proud of my team.

Liam Ives (11)
Whitehill Junior School, Gravesend

Poetry Competition

Frightened is purple like a big sour grape.
Happiness is yellow like a big sunflower.
Sadness is blue like a sparkling sea.
Jealousy is green like the pointy grass.
Anger feels like a pain in your head, which aches.
Anger smells like oil floating in a polluted sea.
Snow is white like a winter's night
Excitement is multicoloured like a rainbow in the sky.

Reece Gregory (11)
Whitehill Junior School, Gravesend

Love

Love is like a red, red rose
That you sprinkle with a little green hose,
When I stand with a pose,
Love is like a red, red rose,
That pops up in the spring,
Love brings joy so that I can sing in the spring.
Love is like a precious thing,
So take good care of it with all your heart
And all your might.
The flower comes in the spring,
The smell comes and goes,
Love is like a red, red rose,
Its taste is ripe,
Its taste is right.
Love is like a red, red rose,
I hear it call,
I hear it shout,
Because love is like a red, red rose.

Tia Tia (11)
Whitehill Junior School, Gravesend

World War II

War looks like thousands of cats fighting
War feels like being hit by a car
War sounds like gun shells hitting the ground.
War smells like dead people in a field.
War tastes like drinking a bottle of hot chilli sauce.

Aaron Merton (10)
Whitehill Junior School, Gravesend

Ouch!

The player's boot's kicking me
I'm flying up in the air,
Now I can see the whole pitch,
The bright blue boot trying to kick me again,
He hit me very hard,
I feel like I have brain damage,
I probably have!

I can hear men calling for the ball,
The fans screaming their heads off,
Men celebrating when they score a goal,
When they score, I just get stuck in the back of the net,
I can hear the goalkeeper shouting, 'Keeper's ball,'
And the whistle blowing at the end of the match.

I feel a cuddle as the player holds me in his arms,
Suddenly they start kicking me again!
I feel hurt when I get smashed against the post or crossbar,
I wish I wasn't a football!

Nafi Asova (11)
Whitehill Junior School, Gravesend

War!

I am stuck in the trench.
Muddy, damp and cramped.
I feel lonely and sad.
Suddenly there is an order,
'Get over the top!'
'Charge!'
I am going to die!
Terrified, my shaking heart thumping,
I jump into the enemy trench.

Jimmy Acott (10)
Whitehill Junior School, Gravesend

My Ferrari

The garage door's open.

You see a lovely red Ferrari,
Look at the tyre tracks up the road,
Watch the red blur go.

Hear exhaust pipes roaring,
Hear tyres squeaking,
Hear the engine revving.

Feel the acceleration,
Feel the engine popping out,
Feel the excitement.

Smell the pollution,
Smell the smoke from tyres,
Smell the polish.

Dream of winning world championships,
Dream of your car going faster.

Hope for a good driver.

Jordan Weller (11)
Whitehill Junior School, Gravesend

War!

War is like thousands of people fighting for their country,
War feels like you're trapped in no-man's-land
War smells like smoke coming out of gun shells.
War sounds like soldiers shouting and guns going off.
War tastes like mud when you take cover from enemy fire.

Chris Trimming (11)
Whitehill Junior School, Gravesend

Feelings

Excitement is multicoloured,
Like a twinkling, glittery rainbow!

Frightened is black,
Like a murky, gloomy tunnel!

Tearful is blue,
Like a swimming pool swaying around!

Bravery is silver,
Like a lucky, shiny ring!

Anger is red,
Like a scorching sun moving around, getting annoyed!

Boredom is grey,
Like a dim, thundery day!

Love is pink,
Like a sunset awakening the evening!

Joyful is gold,
Like a pot of treasure at the end of the rainbow!

Chantelle Pink (11)
Whitehill Junior School, Gravesend

The Simpsons

Homer's bulging belly,
Feels like jelly.
Bart wins an award
By doing tricks on his skateboard.
Marge's blue hair, to brush, is a nightmare.
Lisa studying all the time,
Working till nine.
Bart's spiky hair,
Sticks up in the air.
Maggie sucks her dummy,
Because she wants her mummy.

Daniel Singer (10)
Whitehill Junior School, Gravesend

Jane Seymour

What can you see?

I can see doctors fussing over me.
I can see my door and how much I want to go.
I can see the insides of my eyelids as I slowly drift away.

What can you hear?

I can hear doctors talking, saying it's not good,
I can hear myself breathing deeply,
I can hear my baby screaming.

What can you feel?

I can feel my heart pounding as I take my last breath,
I'm nothing, then I realise . . .
I'm dead.

Charlotte Evans (10)
Whitehill Junior School, Gravesend

Life In A Hutch

In my hutch
I am munching on a carrot
While squeaking.

I can feel furry things,
Good things,
Slushy things,
Spiky things too.

I dream of flowers,
Colourful things,
Girlie things,
Fluffy things.

I hope for *happiness.*

Jordan Vilday (10)
Whitehill Junior School, Gravesend

Feelings Of Catherine Parr

What can you see?

I can see my husband being buried in a huge hole.
I can see my black dress with my leather gloves too.
I can see his children crying and throwing flowers onto his grave.

What can you feel?

I can feel the rough dirt beneath my feet.
I can feel my shoes moving when I walk.
I can feel myself shivering when the breeze blows.

What can you hear?

I can hear the vicar saying our prayers.
I can hear the wind whistling in my ear.
I can hear the gravel being put slowly onto his grave as I walk away.

Now I know what happens next,
Soon, it will be my turn.

Hanna Holloway (10)
Whitehill Junior School, Gravesend

Football Crazy!

It's going to be a good match.

What can you see?
Football players kicking the white ball into the goal,
Players shaking hands before the game begins,
And ref getting ready.

What can you hear?
The crowd shouting their heads off,
For the match to begin and waiting for a goal
To come along for Arsenal!

What do you feel?
The wind zooming into your face,
Blowing you away but you're trying to get in there,
But it hurts when you try.

Louis Gatehouse (11)
Whitehill Junior School, Gravesend

D-Day

What can you see?

Redness like the setting sun in the field of lost lives,
Blackness like the smoke from the bombs.
Brownness like the soldier's uniform
Blue like the sea with a thousand ships sailing on it.

What can you hear?

The sounds of planes crashing into the ocean
The sounds of my friends shouting for cover
Sounds of bombs exploding all around me
I hear my friends fighting for their lives.

What can I feel?

The bullets piercing through my friend's skin
I feel burning in my heart
The fear of dying is burning in my soul.

James Durrant (10)
Whitehill Junior School, Gravesend

World War I

What can you see?

I can see the choking city turning to rubble!
I can see German planes pounding our trenches.
I can see the dead and the wounded struggling to return to the trench

What can you feel?

I can feel the ground shuddering as shells hit no-man's-land!
I can feel my rifle clenched close to my chest.
I can feel the wet, damp mud seeping into my boots.

What can you hear?

I can hear the bombing of the cities nearby!
I can hear the Germans charging fiercely towards us.
I can hear sudden stuttering from machine-gun fire.

Matthew Bagshaw (10)
Whitehill Junior School, Gravesend

Colour Emotions!

Bravery looks like a forceful sword that fights its way to happiness.
Bravery feels like smooth diamonds all in my hands,
not a piece of nastiness.
Bravery tastes like a yummy, sweet milkshake zooming
down my throat following its way.
Bravery smells like the fresh air on the beach and with the lovely
golden sand to lay.
Bravery sounds like the lovely hot sun coming in May.
Excitement smells like a multicoloured bouquet of pretty flowers.
Excitement feels like a thrilling trip to Alton Towers.
Excitement feels like winning the race with all my powers.
Excitement sounds like a whiz-bang firework zooming up in
the sky, not calm!
Excitement tastes like lovely fried eggs in the morning
from a friendly hen on a farm!
Tearful feels like a sapphire, rotten falcon, which flies high.
Tearful looks like miserable rain falling from the sky.
Tearful tastes like bitter coffee, definitely not like a delicious pie.
Tearful smells like burning rubber, burning away on a patch of grass.
Tearful sounds like Concorde blasting off at last.

Yasmin Ullah (10)
Whitehill Junior School, Gravesend

Emotions And Colours

Boredom is grey like a blank screen in a cinema.
Happiness is yellow, like a chick hatching from an egg.
Excitement is multicoloured like a fruit bowl in the sun.
Anger is red like a furnace burning wood.
Tearful is blue like rain falling in the sea.
Bravery is silver like the lining of a cloud.

Melissa Wright (11)
Whitehill Junior School, Gravesend

As I Sank To The Bottom Of The Ocean

As I sank to the bottom of the ocean,
I hoped my husband would be safe,
But I dreamt that he was still floating around the lifeless bodies
surrounding me,
Sinking deeper and deeper.

The ice pierced into my heart and lungs,
The Titanic seemed to be pointing to Heaven,
I could hear shouting and a bright light was passing through
all the bodies,
Searching for me.

As I swam through the murky waters,
I suddenly became desperate.
A high-pitched shriek came bolting out of my mouth,
They had found me at last.

As I rowed away from the 'Queen Of The Ocean',
I still searched for him.
Searching and searching thus was hard, for the night
was as black as coal
But he was submerged.

Clare Stevens (11)
Whitehill Junior School, Gravesend

Senses And Colours

Jealousy sounds like nails being scraped along the blackboard,
Cheerfulness smells like elegant lavender, blooming in the hot sun,
Sadness looks like a wilting oak tree in the cold autumn,
Joy tastes like plump and ripe strawberries sprinkled with sugar,
And love feels like royal-red velvet,
Bravery is silver like a dull, rainy day,
Boredom is grey like a cracked and wonky coffin,
Heaven is white like a flock of sheep.

Julia Johnson (10)
Whitehill Junior School, Gravesend

The Victorian Coal Miner

What can you see?
　　　　I can see black, dusty, old coal,
　　　I can see the roof falling in on me,
　　I can see other children working just like me,
I can see my scaly, old, dusty hands and knees.

What can you hear?
　　　　I can hear the roof crumbling away,
　　　I can hear hammers hitting walls all around,
　　I can hear my head scraping across the ceiling,
I can hear our horrible old boss shouting at us.

What can you feel?
　　　I can feel my head crunching and scraping across the ceiling,
　　　I can feel the darkness of the black, sooty walls
　　I can feel my hands and knees bleeding,
I can feel earth falling on top of me.

Kirsty Williams (11)
Whitehill Junior School, Gravesend

Emotions

Sadness is blue like the deepest, darkest sea,
Jealousy is green like a raw, shrivelled up pea.
Happiness is yellow like a very ripe banana,
Excitement is multicoloured like a camouflaging iguana.
Anger is red like an ever-burning flame,
Heartbroken is black like a panther, not free but tame.
Joy is gold like holding the solid metal,
Cheerful is lilac like a lovely flower's petal.
Boredom is grey like a cloudy thunderstorm,
Tearful is blue like mourning in the morn.
Bravery is silver like a knight in shining armour.
Love is golden like a necklace full of glamour.

Liam Hall-Shelton (10)
Whitehill Junior School, Gravesend

What Are Colours?

What is black?
A mole is black,
Slithering through the underground cracks.

What is white?
A snowflake is white,
Falling joyfully through the night.

What is terracotta?
A mouldy orange is terracotta,
Sitting in the sun getting warmer and hotter.

What is red?
Jam is red,
In cakes and scones and on my bread.

What is emerald?
A bogey is emerald,
Gooey and green from a gobbling that's bold.

Damien Gould (11)
Whitehill Junior School, Gravesend

WWII

I dive into my damp trench,
It's damp like a lake.

I stare into no-man's-land,
It's blank like a turned off TV screen.

I wait to hear the words, 'We won, we won,'
But all I hear are the shouts and screams of men
Coming back from the front row.

I can see our planes charging through their defences.
Like a rhino ramming through a flock of birds.

Finally we hear the words, 'We've won!' and we cheer like never
before.

Tom Coates (11)
Whitehill Junior School, Gravesend

The Victorian Chimney Sweep

What can you see?

I can see shiny sparks flickering at the bottom.
I can see a very dull light at the top of the chimney.
I can see dirty black soot falling to the ground.

What can you feel?

I can feel the slimy bricks in my hands.
I can feel the webs clinging to me as I go past them.
I can feel the wind smacking me like an angry woman.

What can you hear?

I can hear my sweat dripping madly.
I can hear the fire crackling a bit.
I can hear my boss shouting for me to go higher.

Kelly Jackson (11)
Whitehill Junior School, Gravesend

Sparkling Rainbow

Anger is red,
Like a tomato in the hands of a criminal.

Happiness is yellow,
Like a hot sunny day.

Frightened is black,
Like a deep, dark tunnel.

Sadness is blue,
Like coming to school on a Monday morning.

Excitement is multicoloured,
Like a sparkling rainbow.

Boredom is grey,
Like a blank TV screen.

Sam Nichols (11)
Whitehill Junior School, Gravesend

Flying Football

I see tall football players surrounding me,
After 10 mins they all smash me.
I see me smacked against a goalpost,
When I come down
I start bouncing the most.

I hear the crowd whistling for full time,
The goals they score are always sublime.
I fly and walk almost every day,
I never get kicked the fourth week in May.

I always feel dirty,
When they kick me,
Then I feel sick,
When they kiss me.

I'm always kicked,
I'm always flicked,
The ref's in black,
And penalties are a lack.

Wishing I was never a football
But I have no choice,
I will always be a round football.

Kenneth Hyde (11)
Whitehill Junior School, Gravesend

Anne Boleyn's Beheading

As I walk up the rickety old steps to the platform,
My heart is beating fast.
Tears are forming in my eyes,
Though I must not let them see me that way.

My people that adored me,
Seem to not care.
I am dressed in my best outfit,
This time, no one's looking at it.

The mindless chatter that fills the air around me,
I cannot help but feel,
Is my only form of comfort.
As Henry is not here.

I am just about to reach the place I dread.
I suppose nothing can help me now,
I am kneeling down and my sleeve is caught on something.
My fingers are revealed.

I place my head carefully in the dip.
The executioner is sharpening his blade.
Worried, I begin to say my prayers.
And before I am finished . . .
Chop!

Olivia Steen (11)
Whitehill Junior School, Gravesend